JOHN ANKERBERG
DILLON BURROUGHS

Middle East Meltdown

HARVEST HOUSE PUBLISHERS

EUGENE, OREGON

Cover by Terry Dugan Design, Minneapolis, Minnesota

Cover photo © Terry J. Alcorn / iStockphoto

Back cover author photo of Dillon Burroughs © Goldberg Photography

MIDDLE EAST MELTDOWN
Copyright © 2007 by John Ankerberg and Dillon Burroughs
Published by Harvest House Publishers
Eugene, Oregon 97402
www.harvesthousepublishers.com

Library of Congress Cataloging-in-Publication Data
  Ankerberg, John, 1945-
  Middle East meltdown / John Ankerberg and Dillon Burroughs.
    p. cm.
  ISBN-13: 978-0-7369-2119-0 (pbk.)
  ISBN-10: 0-7369-2119-2
  1. Bible—Prophecies—Middle East. 2. Eschatology. 3. Middle East—History—Prophecies.
4. Middle East—Forecasting. I. Burroughs, Dillon. II. Title.
  BS649.N45A55 2007
  236.'9—dc22
                                                                                        2006034082

Printed in the United States of America

07 08 09 10 11 12 13 14 15 / VP-SK / 10 9 8 7 6 5 4 3 2 1

*"There is nothing worse than religious war,
because people are so convinced that they are right."*

SUSAN TOLCHIN[1]

CONTENTS

Five Reasons You Should Read This Book Now

A plot against airlines.
Osama bin Laden at large.
Iraq in flames.
Five years after 9/11,
are we any safer?

The week following the foiled London-airline terror plot, *Newsweek*'s cover posed the following key question: *Are we any safer?*

In the years since 9/11, our world has changed dramatically. We now live in a new world where the terrorist actions of religious zealots have become the norm. Today Wall Street finds itself surrounded by officers with machine guns, airlines inspect passengers' shoes for fear of shoe bombs, and passengers have even been required to throw away bottled water as a potential safety threat. CNN, FOX News, MSNBC, and the major networks daily update us on the most recent terror threats. *Is the threat level yellow or orange today? How early will I need to arrive at the airport? Who was bombed this time?*

Nearly every day a new flight security alert hits the airwaves. One recent CBS newscast began with the shocking headline of not one, but *seven,* airline security scares in one day:

> A tense day Friday in the air with seven security scares in planes. Among the incidents, a Connecticut college student now faces federal charges after a bomb-sniffing dog found a stick of dynamite in his luggage in Houston. Officials say it was not an act of terrorism.

On a US Airways flight a man was subdued by a federal air marshal and the jet was forced to land in Oklahoma City.

And a flight from New York to Dublin was evacuated in Western Ireland because of a bomb threat.[2]

We care for our children, our spouse, our friends, and our families. We long for a time of peace. Yet today's headlines reveal we live in an increasingly chaotic world. The most-discussed articles at Newsweek.com during a recent week included:

- Are These the End Times?
- How Bush Makes Enemies
- Why the U.S. Is Letting Lebanon Bleed

Not very encouraging, is it? In addition to acts of terror at home, we continue to face civil strife in Iraq, battles on both sides of Israel, a defiant Iran at work toward nuclear weapons, nuclear threats from North Korea, and a growing worldwide resentment toward the United States. Politicians argue, religious leaders warn that Armageddon is near, corporate leaders worry about the changing economy, and the everyday person seeks answers to what is happening on the world scene today. Ultimately, many of us simply want to know, *Will it ever be the same again?*

While this book will touch on many of the political and economic factors at play in the War on Terror, its primary emphasis is *spiritual*. While that may not seem all that urgent or newsworthy, in actuality, it is. In fact, there are five reasons we believe *every* person should read this book today:

1. You need to know *why* this conflict is happening.

Few people truly understand the nature of the Middle East conflict behind the acts of terror at Ground Zero and beyond. Even our top intelligence and military leaders have frequently underestimated the religious convictions that are driving the evil regimes of our world. For instance, did you know that the recent threat to destroy Chicago's Sears Tower originated from a religious movement called the "Seas of David," a group that blends various aspects of radical Islam and Christianity?[3] How many in the public realize that the Islamic concept of jihad (holy war) is not just an extremist viewpoint, but a foundational concept from the earliest times of the Muslim religion? Most Americans would find themselves equally shocked to discover that an orthodox Jewish movement has already prepared enormous cornerstones for the future temple to be rebuilt at the Dome of the Rock in Jerusalem, along with thousands of detailed pieces of clothing, musical instruments, and tools for worship.[4]

Even domestic issues such as the politically charged controversy over immigration are at least in part based on concerns about terrorism. For instance, on June 6, 2006, the following story became public:

> Yet again, fiction seems to have a way of foreshadowing reality. Canadian authorities arrested 17 people whom they allege are part of a radical Islamic terror cell planning major attacks throughout the U.S. and Canada.[5]

The same concern was recently shared on Fox's *Hannity & Colmes* program during an interview with Pat Buchanan regarding his book *State of Emergency*. The conversation, though focused primarily on Mexican immigration, later turned toward issues of terrorism:

> **HANNITY:** Here we are. We're at the fifth anniversary of 9/11. The biggest area of susceptibility we have is at our borders for our enemies coming across, still wide open. If Al Qaeda members want to cross our border, they're free to do so, aren't they?
>
> **BUCHANAN:** They said they're going to do it. And we're catching more and more folks who are not from Mexico at all but from the Middle East and Asia. We don't know who they are. Under the "catch-and-release" policy the president had, three in four are turned loose in our society and never turn up in court.[6]

Even today's nuclear disputes result from strongly held religious beliefs. For instance, Iran's development of weapons of mass destruction in defiance of U.N. Resolution 1696[7] has been strongly backed by its prime minister's plan to wage war against "the little Satan" (Israel) and "the big Satan" (the United States). These weapons have little to do with self-defense or national security. The roots of these actions are ultimately *spiritual*.

Middle East Meltdown will help you understand the part religion plays in all that is happening today. Judaism, Christianity, and Islam all enter the picture, and before anyone can come up with enduring solutions, we have to recognize that the problems, at heart, are spiritual.

2. You need to know *what's* really happening.

> *"America is at war."*
>
> U.S. President George Bush,
> the first sentence of the 2006 National Security Strategy paper[8]

Almost every day, I (Dillon) find myself in a conversation with someone who says, "I can't stand to watch the news anymore. I usually just change the channel." While the graphic nature of today's news or the strong opinions of certain personalities may make this an understandable response at times, the unfortunate consequence is that the average American has little understanding of today's Middle East conflict. The "Roadmap for Peace" in the Middle East might as well be a map in your glove compartment! There is simply so much bad news that many choose to hear no news at all.

If you could read a brief book that would help you better understand the factors at play in the War on Terror without sensationalism (and without commercials!), wouldn't you consider it worth your time? *Middle East Meltdown* intends to help you grasp the big picture of key Middle Eastern issues and today's terrorist attacks in a user-friendly way that hits the essentials, including the Bible's perspective, without overwhelming you with an endless number of details or opinions.

3. You need to know *where* this conflict is headed.

In addition to understanding *why* this conflict is taking place and *what's* happening in the War on Terror, it's critical to look ahead at *where* the conflict is headed. Why are the Hezbollah in conflict with

Israel? Why does Iran want nuclear weapons? Why is Iran promising to share this technology with other Arab nations?

If you could be shown some of the major upcoming concerns about the conflict and terrorism *before* they happened, wouldn't you be interested in knowing more? While we make no promise to predict the future, an analysis of the recent progression of events helps us to point where events are most likely to take place in the days ahead. You might even find yourself reading some of tomorrow's headlines *today*.

4. You need to know *what* the Bible teaches about today's War on Terror.

As Christians, we hold dearly to what the Bible says on all issues, especially on today's hotly charged topics of terrorism and the Middle-East conflict. Building on over 25 years of interviewing the top religious scholars in biblical prophecy, church history, theology, and comparative religions, a major portion of this book shares insightful views of how the Bible connects with the war in Iraq, rising anti-Americanism in the Middle East, and God's future for Israel. You may be surprised at how much the Bible really *does* say about today's events and how accurately the Bible's predictions have been fulfilled over the years.

It's interesting to note that even some of today's top novels build upon the teachings found in the Christian and Jewish Scriptures. For instance, Dr. Joel Rosenberg's best-selling novel, *The Ezekiel Option*, describes how the events of Ezekiel 38–39 could play out in conjunction with today's Middle East politics. Beginning in the mid-1990s Dr. Tim LaHaye and Jerry Jenkins offered the world their take on the rapture in what we now know as the *Left Behind*® series. It has become the best-selling fiction series in history, with well over 63 million books sold. Their novels provide a contemporary take on the predictions the Bible has made about the rapture, a future one-world government, and the battles of the last days.

Middle East Meltdown will not only guide you through today's War on Terror; it will guide you through the Bible's perspective on today's conflicts. We'll share directly from God's Word so you can evaluate for yourself how it applies to today's events.

5. You need to know *how to respond* to today's War on Terror.

Because we are all affected by the War on Terror, we all need tools and tips for living life in light of today's realities. Though Americans displayed a strong religious response following the events of 9/11, studies show that five years later, the faith of Americans is "virtually indistinguishable today compared to pre-attack conditions. Barna's tracking surveys looked at 19 dimensions of spirituality and beliefs. Remarkably, none of those 19 indicators are statistically different from the summer before the attacks!"[9] Why is this happening?

Middle East Meltdown will provide you with information for both personal reflection and practical application. By the time you finish reading these pages, you will not only know many new facts, but you will also discover practical ways to get involved in education and aid, and find a personal spiritual challenge for preparation in today's world *and* for eternity.

Our desire is not only to influence your *thinking;* we desire to influence your *living.* These pages are written for you as a mom or dad, student, teacher, lawyer, nurse, barista, waitress, engineer, insurance rep, business executive, soldier, government official, or spiritual leader to become a better individual and build a better tomorrow through the principles learned and applied from *Middle East Meltdown.*

1

Imagine a Day...

*"The principal failure to act to prevent the September 11
attack was a "failure of imagination." A failure of
imagination leads many today to discount the risk of
a nuclear 9/11...Al Qaeda has tried to acquire or make
nuclear weapons for at least 10 years...and continues to
pursue its strategic goal of obtaining a nuclear capability."* [10]

BULLETIN OF THE ATOMIC SCIENTISTS

AP News reports, "We have just learned of a new development in Iran. Less than ten minutes ago, a Shahab-3 missile was fired from Northern Iran, near a site blocked from U.N. inspectors for over three years, according to reports from the Pentagon. No other details were released, but an unnamed source has confirmed the target appears to be somewhere in Israel, perhaps toward Old Jerusalem itself. Whether the missile is nuclear or not has not been revealed, but Israeli military are already beginning to take action as IDF air forces are preparing for a retaliatory strike...."

"CNN reporting...this just in: Iran has just fired a Shahab missile toward Israel in an unprecedented attack. Pentagon officials have yet to release details, but many are concerned this may be a *nuclear* strike. IDF forces are already beginning counterattacks, according to Israeli news sources. The president is scheduled to speak in an upcoming news conference to update the nation on these new activities. Of course, we'll be following all of the action here, so stay tuned for more. Let's turn to our analyst...."

"This just in at FOX News: Iran's Ahmadinejad has led a missile attack on Israel. Little information is available at the moment, but FOX has learned this is likely a Shahab-3 missile, one of the missiles the U.N. has been concerned about due to its ability to carry a nuclear warhead. Israeli defense forces are currently being deployed in response and American military personnel are on heightened alert. We're looking now for information regarding the specific direction of the missile and updates on what missile defense is in place for a response. An upcoming news conference is coming with further details. Moving now to our correspondent in Tel Aviv...."

"ABC News has just learned that an Iranian missile has been launched toward the nation of Israel. The Pentagon has yet to release additional information, but Israeli and American military forces are already on alert. Of major concern is whether this alleged Shahab-3 missile is carrying a nuclear warhead, a concern for some time, as Iran's president has threatened since 2005 to 'wipe Israel off the map.' The following satellite video shows the initial launch and current pattern...."

The above reports are *fictional* accounts. Though they didn't actually happen, the problem is that such news is closer to reality than we think. Whether from Iran, as portrayed here, or via the terrorist activities of al-Qaeda, Hezbollah, Hamas, or another radical movement, a very real fear exists of similar actions taking place at any time in our world. Leading scientists, military strategists, politicians, and spiritual experts are increasingly warning against the possibility of a world-changing attack on Israel, America, or European nations.

In fact, on the first page of its founding manifesto, the massively funded Department of Homeland Security intones, "Today's terrorists can strike at any place, at any time, and *with virtually any weapon*" (emphasis added).[11]

In its review of the intelligence concerns in relation to the attacks on 9/11, the *9/11 Commission Report* stated that the greatest failure in preventing the death of over 3,000 Americans on September 11, 2001 was not a lack of *intelligence;* it was a lack of *imagination.* The same can be said today. One of our greatest weaknesses is that we fail to imagine such a disaster could take place. We want to believe our personal lives, our families, our careers, our community, and our world will continue to offer an ongoing blanket of security for everyday living. We do not want to accept the reality that our world is no longer safe. We want to turn off the news reports rather than acknowledge that new attacks could happen at any time in any place.

Not only do we need to be realistic about what could happen, but we also need to realize that *religious* beliefs are driving the violence. For instance, did you know:

- Osama bin Laden, Ayman al-Zawahiri, and many other Islamic leaders, both radical and nonradical, are calling for the recreation of an Islamic Caliphate consisting of all 1.5 billion Muslims in the world? This is nothing short of *an allied jihad* of violence against the non-Muslim world.

- the president of Iran believes he is the forerunner of the Islamic Messiah and has called for *the eradication of Israel?*

- the Bible predicts Syria, Egypt, Iran, Turkey, Libya, Sudan, and Russia will form alliances with one another and *come against Israel* in the last days? An ancient biblical text of 3,000 years ago describes these nations:

  With cunning they conspire against your people; they plot against those you cherish. "Come," they say, "let us destroy them as a nation, *that the name of Israel be remembered no more.*" With one mind they plot together; they form an alliance against you (Psalm 83:3-5).

As we journey through these pages, we'll discover that God's Word is not silent about what is happening. Rather, much of what we see today was predicted with amazing accuracy centuries ago. Not only can we "imagine" what will take place, but we will find that God has a specific plan in place for the world—a plan that coincides with today's activities in remarkable ways.

2

Setting the Stage

"Our world will never be the same."

U.S. President George W. Bush, regarding 9/11

Everybody remembers where they were when they first heard about the horrific attacks of September 11, 2001.[12] I (John) had spent a vacation with my family in New York City only days before the attacks. We shopped in Manhattan, watched a play, stayed at the Hilton off of Park Avenue, and enjoyed meals at some of the magnificent restaurants found only in the Big Apple. One evening during our trip, we toured the top of the Empire State Building, viewing the city skyline from a breathtaking location. Along that skyline stood the distinctive twin towers, the architectural masterpiece of one of America's greatest cities.

A few days later in Tennessee, I was in the middle of producing an upcoming episode of our television program when my wife Darlene interrupted. "John, you'd better come see this. An airplane just flew into the side of one of the twin towers." At first, I thought there must have been some kind of mistake. We had *just been there.* Everything *had* to be okay.

As I walked into another room to watch the coverage, my wife and I viewed a growing cloud of smoke in the background as the newscaster continued his comments. The viewing audience saw it before the broadcasters did. One of the world's tallest buildings, one I had just observed up close with my family, holding thousands of other working family members, crumbled live before a worldwide audience. *I knew then our world would never be the same.*

On that day, I (Dillon) was attending a graduate lecture on church history. The professor mentioned a plane crash had happened, but the details were sketchy. A couple of minutes later, I politely slipped out, concerned that something big was happening. I jogged across the campus square, into the library computer lab, and logged onto CNN. *No access.* I tried FOX News. *Server too busy.* I kept reloading different news sites until I finally got through to MSNBC's home page. As the page loaded, the first thing I saw was rolling smoke from one of the Twin Towers. Shocked, I kept reading to find out more. *I soon realized that what I first saw was only the beginning.*

Using four jetliners, Islamic terrorists struck the twin towers of the World Trade Center and the Pentagon. One of the jets was brought down in a field near Shanksville, Pennsylvania. The attacks killed nearly 3,000 people and left the name Ground Zero etched into the minds of Americans who frightfully watched the events of that horrific day unfold.

Five years later, fears of a similar disaster simmer in the minds of all Americans. Unfortunately, today's headlines have provided little to settle our concerns. An August 2006 *Newsweek* article titled "Terror in Our Time" listed a progression of terrorist attacks and major threats since the world's turning point at 9/11. A few excerpts include:

- April 11, 2002: Truck bomb explodes outside a synagogue in Tunisia.

- June 14, 2002: Car-bomber attacks American Consulate building in Karachi, Pakistan, killing 11 people.

- March 11, 2004: In a sophisticated attack, terrorists set off bombs in four crowded Madrid commuter trains...191 people are killed and more than 1,700 are injured.

- August 11, 2006: British authorities uncover an alleged plot
  to explode bombs on ten airliners traveling from Britain
  to the United States. The alleged bombers would smuggle
  liquid explosives onboard disguised as beverages and other
  common objects. Twenty-four people are detained for questioning.[13]

Is Hope for Peace Realistic?

Shortly following the events of 9/11, I (John) gathered some
prophecy scholars for a television broadcast about world events in
light of biblical prophecy.[14] I interviewed news correspondent Dr.
Jimmy DeYoung, a man who had spent over a decade reporting on
location in Israel interviewing every Israeli prime minister since
1991. During our time together, I asked him, "The Israeli-Arab conflict has been raging for over fifty years. Suicide bombers, brutal
attacks, and reprisals are causing many people to wonder, 'Is peace
possible in the Middle East?'"

Dr. DeYoung instantly responded, "I believe that we're at a spot
in history when there is no way there is going to be peace between
the Palestinians and the Israelis. The Palestinians want war." He continued to explain, saying, "Now, the Bible says all of that. I'm telling
you what current events are in reality, but God's Word prophesied
over 2,500 years ago that this is the situation we'd be in during the
end times when all these nations want to go against Israel and wipe
it off the face of the earth."

During the first Gulf War in 1991, we taped a television broadcast with over 4,000 people in attendance at the Peabody Hotel in
Orlando, Florida. Best-selling author Hal Lindsey made an eerily
similar comment as Dr. DeYoung, saying, "I believe that the Bible
is very clear that the last war of the world will start with a war over
Jerusalem…the whole centerpiece of the prophetic scenario rests
around the nation of Israel.

"There are three things the Bible predicted would happen to the
people of Israel just shortly before the return of Christ. First, there
would be the miraculous rebirth of the state of Israel physically.

Second, they would recapture old Jerusalem and have sovereign control over it. Third, they will rebuild the temple."

He then reflected on what other Christian scholars had noted regarding Israel over the last 350 years. "It's extraordinary that in the 1800s there was a great resurgence of interest in prophecy. People began to categorize it and take it literally, especially in England and Scotland. There were many in those days who began to say certain things that indicated they believed that prophecy would soon be fulfilled. For instance:

- In 1864, Dr. John Cummings said, 'As a nation they were cut off and dispersed and it is as a nation that *Israel shall be gathered and restored again.*' In that time no one believed it was possible.

- In 1866, James Grant said, 'The personal coming of Christ to establish his thousand-year reign on earth will not take place until the Jews are restored to their land, the enemies of Christ and the Jews have been gathered together, and their armies from all parts of the world gather and besiege Jerusalem and are destroyed.'

- In 1669, a Colonial preacher in New England, Increase Mather, said in his book *The Mystery of Israel's Salvation* that Israel would have to be reborn in the last days. This was impossible in his time. Israel was scattered throughout the world and persecuted from Russia all the way around to Morocco."

Amazingly, when Cummings, Grant, and Mather made their statements, the people of Israel were scattered worldwide and the nation did not exist. These writers based their conclusions solely on Bible prophecy.

The Conflict Rages

Dave Hunt, founder of The Berean Call and a best-selling author with over four million books in print, excitedly interjected at this point. "In Zechariah 12, God said, 'In the last days I am going to make Jerusalem a cup of trembling for all nations...a burdensome stone to all the peoples.'"

Dr. David Breese provided an additional personal insight: "I'll never forget a conversation I had in the Knesset once upon a time as I talked with an Israeli leader. We finished with the military situation, and he said to me, 'Dave, remember something. In the battles of the Middle East, the Arabs could lose many times and still come back. *We can only lose once and it is all over.*' Then he said, 'To be or not to be, that is the question!' Well, if the question is to be or not to be, then you cannot afford many diplomatic niceties. They have to decide *now* what to do about any threat.

"It's possible for the Israeli chiefs of staff to meet at midnight and then the Israeli air force to fly by 4:00 A.M. They are the most instantly responsive military force in the world. The reason is because the question with Israel is not, 'What do you do to please the world?' or 'How do you get along with the diplomats of the world?' but the question is, 'How can we survive?' When you are facing a person for whom the question is survival, all of the other niceties may be nice but they don't mean a thing."

I also asked Dave Hunt, "Why does the Arab world want to overthrow and destroy Israel?"

Dave replied, "Yasser Arafat's uncle, who used to be the grand mufti of Jerusalem, fled to Germany. Over Radio Berlin during the Second World War, he said to the Arabs, 'Rise as one man and kill the Jews wherever you find them. This pleases God and religion and God is with you.' Arafat says, 'Our struggle with Israel is such that when it is finished, Israel will cease to exist. There can be no compromise.'" According to Dave, the violence is deeply rooted in history and theology.

The Conflict over the Temple Mount

The events of the past decade have made the words of another interview I (John) conducted with Jimmy DeYoung feel increasingly relevant today. In 1996, during a brief return to the United States from Israel, he commented, "In the infrastructure of Israel itself you have Islamic jihad and you have Hamas. Their stated goal is, 'We want to rid the world of the Jewish people and we'll do that if we have to do it in bits and pieces.' Yasser Arafat was basically calling for Islamic jihad. He was calling for *war*."

It was during this time that Dr. DeYoung shared with me an interesting story about his coverage of the Israel-Jordanian peace agreement: "In 1994, Bill Clinton came for his first visit to Israel. He came and they signed the peace agreement between Israel and Jordan. Afterwards he came into Jerusalem. As a journalist I was covering this situation and Bill Clinton said he wanted to go into the old city and visit the Temple Mount. He had never been there and wanted to do some sightseeing.

"When he said that, Yasser Arafat replied, 'You will not take him up there! Nobody will take him up there!' They locked every single gate to the Temple Mount. They put armed Palestinian guards behind them. Yasser Arafat made the statement, 'Nobody goes on the Temple Mount unless I take them up there and do the tour with them.' This man had become intoxicated with power to control Jerusalem, the most important spot on the face of the earth for the Jewish people."

What About Jerusalem?

During this same interview, I asked DeYoung about his future concerns over Jerusalem. He responded, "There's going to be an unbelievable conflict. I was at the celebration when they kicked off the three-thousandth anniversary of the city of Jerusalem being named not only the political capital but the spiritual capital of the Jewish people in October 1995. Go back to Second Samuel five and you'll see that King David, moving from Hebron, came to Jerusalem, and was established as the king of all the Jewish people, and he needed a capital city. He chose the Jebuzite stronghold, the city of Jerusalem, and he established it.

"On the other side of the coin, we hear Palestinian leadership saying Jerusalem is going to be *their* capital for the Palestinian state. The mufti said, 'It is very important as far as our religiosity is concerned.' It's the third most sacred city as far as the Muslims are concerned: Mecca, Medina, and then Jerusalem.

"But the Qur'an, the holy book for the Muslim people, never mentions the city of Jerusalem. It never says a word about Muhammad coming to the city of Jerusalem. Within the last 150 years, political decisions have moved Palestinians to saying this is an important city as far as our religion and as far as our existence is concerned."

It is clear from what has been said that the Palestinians and Israelis will never change their positions regarding the fundamental issue of whom Jerusalem belongs to.

Plans for a New Temple

Gershon Salomon is the leader and chairman of the Temple Mount Faithful movement in Israel.[15] On October 8, 1990, he led a procession of Jewish people to the Temple Mount and attempted to bring the cornerstone for what would be the Third Temple. This sparked a Palestinian riot that drew worldwide attention and resulted in the United Nations condemning Israel and Saddam Hussein firing SCUD missiles against Israel during the Gulf War. But concerning the rebuilding of the temple, Gershon told me (John) with confidence, "I have no doubt that you and I, we shall see the Ark of the Covenant in the middle of the Third Temple on the Temple Mount in Jerusalem very soon—in our lifetime."

In a 2002 interview with archaeologist Dr. Randall Price, who lived and worked in Jerusalem for several years, I asked, "Are there really plans underway in Israel to rebuild the Jewish Temple?"

He answered, "When I began the research for one of my books, I was of the opinion that this was simply a radical grassroots or fanatical movement that was taking place in Israel. But the more I got behind the scenes, the more I saw that it was not only the secular Jews who were interested in the temple as a national monument, it was also the religious leaders who were very active in the process. Today, in Israel, we see implements being prepared for the actual conduct of sacrificial worship. We find vestments being made for the priests. There is even a training school called *Ateret Cohanim* where young men are being prepared for the actual function of the priesthood. They declare that they expect in their lifetime to actually fulfill that kind of function. We see that a site has been located for the temple. We also see that there are settlements being established all around the Temple Mount. Some of the things that are in the news about establishments of settlements in the city of David and in the Muslim quarter all have behind it the intent of bringing a Jewish presence to the Temple Mount so that when the temple is constructed, people will be in place."

Surprised, I then asked Dr. Price, "Why have we not heard more about these plans from mainstream news sources? What are the politics involved here? Why would some people want to downplay what is happening in Israel?" Dr. Price responded,

"I think the primary reason is because of the great sensitivity connected with this issue. The rebuilding of the temple, and even the Temple Mount itself, has the potential to ignite a conflict in the Middle East of the proportions of a third world war. We have already seen on October 8, 1980, the Temple Mount incident in which there was a stoning of Jewish worshippers and retaliation by the Israeli police. Seventeen Palestinian Arabs were killed. The U.N. condemned Israel. Saddam Hussein used that to say, 'Israel is the real occupier. They're the real aggressors in the Middle East.' He launched SCUD missiles hoping to divert attention from his occupation of Kuwait and draw the United States away from their Arab allies. This kind of thing has that kind of potential."

Dr. Price also commented on the historical Ark of the Covenant, an artifact most of us know primarily from the movie *Raiders of the Lost Ark* rather than from the Bible. Interestingly, Jews believe the Ark will surface during the time of the temple's rebuilding. In Price's book *Ready to Rebuild* is an excerpt from an interview with chief rabbi Yehuda Getz, who said,

> This gate, and the Coponius Gate, a little bit further [north] from it in the Western Wall that we discovered ten years ago is a secret. The big vault that we saw [inside it] is one of the entrances to the Temple. [And as for the Ark of the Covenant], we know exactly where it is![16]

If they knew where the Ark was, why didn't they bring it out of hiding? Apparently because there's no proper place to put it at this time. It must be placed in the temple. The stage has already been set for the Jews to rebuild the temple quickly when the opportunity presents itself—an event that Scripture says will take place someday.

Fast-forward from America's initial recovery in the weeks following 9/11 to today's current events, especially the recently foiled plot in Britain in which terrorists had planned to bomb several London-to-U.S. airplanes. Almost daily we hear media reports of suspicious activity on a plane or in an airport terminal. In fact, today, the following story shot across my (Dillon's) computer monitor: "Disturbance Diverts London-D.C. Flight."[17]

The article stated, "Fighter jets escorted a diverted London-to-Washington, D.C., flight to Boston's Logan Airport Wednesday after a distraught passenger pulled out a screw driver, matches, Vaseline and a note referencing al-Qaida...Transportation Security Administration spokeswoman Amy von Walter said. According to Von Walter, the fighter jets launched and trailed the flight out of an abundance of caution."

This is the new world facing the War on Terror—fighter-escorted flights, plans to rebuild an ancient temple, a growing number of terrorists attacks, and a new awareness that religion drove our history and is driving our present and future.

Part 1

The Past: Foundations for Understanding the Meltdown

"We are going to a clash of civilization. Not a clash of civilizations, but a question of where we are going to be as a world, and the clash literally being between the two greatest evangelistic faiths, those of Islam and Christianity."[18]

DR. ERGUN CANER,
DURING AN INTERVIEW ON *THE JOHN ANKERBERG SHOW*

I (John) can still hear Dr. Caner's words ringing in my ears. As Dillon and I watched the raw video footage of this intriguing interview, we discussed the implications of speaking up about such sensitive information. Though controversial, in the end, we knew that before anyone can truly understand the current Middle East situation, he or she needs to journey through key highlights of religious history. Islam's history, Judaism's origin, and Christianity's influence[19] each offer insightful perspective into the contemporary and future dynamics affecting the meltdown of our times.

Our trek will include interviews with scholars with expertise in each of these areas. First, Dr. Ergun Mehmet Caner and his brother, Dr. Emir Fethi Caner, both former Muslims, were disowned by their family upon becoming Christians. They later pursued their doctoral degrees and now teach at leading Christian universities. They will share about Islam for those unacquainted with its practices and beliefs. Next, Jewish-Christian journalist and expert Dr. Jimmy DeYoung will provide an intriguing insider's view as one who has lived and worked among Israel's top political and spiritual leaders. And third, we will consider the thoughts of eight leading scholars from various academic disciplines as they share about the traditions and theology of Christianity from angles rarely considered in today's churches. Together, these experts will help us explore the foundations of these three major world religions.

3

Islam's Creed: No God but Allah

"The real difference between the two religions, however, lies in their basis for belief. Judaism is based on the unique historical event of a divine revelation experienced by the entire nation, whereas Islam is based on the prophetic claims of a single individual who subsequently convinced others to follow his ways."[20]

"There is no assurance of salvation in the God of the Koran. There is no room for redemption. There is no example of Calvary. Missing totally. And to me, the most marvelous thing is, I find in Jesus Christ an assurance of forgiveness of my sins now, right now. Secondly, I find in Jesus Christ assurance of eternal life now—by trusting Him as One who died for my sins, took my place, atoned for my sins…. in the final analysis, the Koran teaches you…do all the work you can. Fulfill all the five pillars of Islam. And still you have no assurance. God has the prerogative to send you to hell no matter what you've done."[21]

Dr. Anis Shorrosh

In March 2006, I (John) had the unique privilege of interviewing two of today's top Islamic-Christian scholars, Dr. Ergun Mehmet Caner, and his brother, Dr. Emir Fethi Caner. Ergun serves as president of Liberty Theological Seminary in Lynchburg, Virginia, while Emir serves as dean of the college at Southwestern Theological Seminary in Fort Worth, Texas. Combined, they have addressed tens of thousands of individuals, authored best-selling books, and have been featured on major networks such as CNN and NPR and BBC. But what strikes people most when encountering the Caner brothers is not primarily their scholarship, media exposure, or writings, but

KEY MUSLIM PRACTICES

To recite the shahadah: This is the reciting of the creed, "There is no god but Allah, and Muhammad is His messenger."

To pray (salat): This includes 17 prayers per day, prayer at noon at a mosque on Fridays, and five specified times of prayer daily.

To fast (sawm): Muslims refrain from food during the daylight hours during the lunar month of Ramadhan.

To give alms (zakat): Muslims are required to give one fortieth of their income (2.5 percent) to the poor and needy.

To make the pilgrimage (hajj): Those physically and financially able must visit Mecca at least once during their lifetime. The journey usually takes at least a week, including many stops at other holy sites along the way.[22]

their amazing personal stories about their conversion to Christianity out of a devout Muslim family tradition—tradition that even included their own father moving to America to build Islamic mosques.

Because the brothers are researchers and scholars, some people expect they are stuffy guys who would prefer a quiet spot in an academic library. Yet they know how to laugh, have a good time, and enjoy everyday humor—at least until the conversation turns to matters of faith. Then their personalities take on a much more serious look—a look arising from a lifetime of battle over the issues at hand.

Islam 101

As we began our time together, I wanted to start with the basics. Ergun introduced my television audience to the world of Islam, opening with an overview of the main variations between Muslims.

"You have to understand that there are three types of Muslims who come to America. First, there are the *cultural Muslims.* They're just born into Islam, but they're not devout in any way. The *extreme devout,* which we were, are orthodox, and you don't have contact with non-Muslims. Surah 5 of the Qur'an teaches that you 'take no friends from among the Jews and the Christians.' So it's a very isolated community from which we came. The third group of *moderates* is a little friendlier in the communities. When I was a Muslim looking at Christianity, I couldn't understand what a fat man in a red suit had to do with the birth of Jesus. Or what did a bunny or eggs have to do with the resurrection? When we would bring this up, other Muslims would say, 'See, they're even mocking their own religion, because they know that Christianity is a lie.'

"You can summarize the difference between Christianity and Islam in the Islamic mind by saying the Jew had the truth, lost it, and corrupted it. Then the Christian had the truth, lost it, and corrupted it.[23] Then comes Muhammad, the final hope. So he saves us, he protects, and receives from the angel Gabriel the absolute truth, which is Islam. Christianity, Judaism, and all other world systems are seen as ghosts, empty shells of themselves. This was our view. This was what we thought of anything that was Christian."

A Day in the Life of a Muslim

With a desire to understand the daily life of someone raised Muslim, I asked the Caners questions about their personal lives to better comprehend their spiritual background. I began by asking, "People who are listening may not understand that Islam is all-encompassing. It dictates *everything*, every part of your life. Roll me through a day. You wake up in the morning and what happens?"

Ergun instantly illustrated the connection between faith and family. "There are five prayer times through the day. You face Mecca and pray. You begin every activity with the Arabic phrase meaning 'if Allah wills it.' The foods that you eat are *halal* or *haram*, allowable or forbidden. There is also one small little section called *mushbu*, but

---

A CHRISTIAN PRAYER FOR MUSLIMS

We covenant to pray for our Muslim friends,

that they find the Jesus Christ who is...

More than a Messenger...

He is Messiah.

More than a Servant...

He is Savior.

More that the Word of God...

He is God.

More than Virgin Born...

He was Crucified, Buried, and Resurrected.

More than Assumed at Death...

He conquered death and Ascended on High.

More than a Prophet...

He is Prophet, Priest, and King.[24]

those don't count. Like vitamins, they fit in the 'not sure' category. Every day is dictated—the clothes that you wear, the way that you dress, down to the smallest detail of how you address those who are the unbelievers, the infidels.

"The last thing you do and the first thing you do is prayer. But it's not prayer like in the Christian world, where we pray and bring requests. It is *ritual*. You carry this out in obedience, because our day is basically living in constant fear of the scales. The twenty-third chapter of the Qur'an teaches [that] at the end of your life you must have accomplished more good than bad on the scales. So everything we carried out was for the purpose and the hope that it would out-weigh what we had done or thought."

The Muslim View of Heaven

I switched to another personal question, asking specifics about the afterlife. "What was salvation for you in Islam? In other words, to get to paradise or heaven, what were you supposed to do?" Emir's response at this point was not that of an academic, but a person with a passionate concern for people's eternal destiny:

"The pillars of Islam really demonstrate that Islam is a *works-based religion*. Not only reciting the creed, 'There is no God but Allah, and Muhammad is his prophet,' and saying it tens of thousands of times through your life; but the prayers five times daily; the fasting which is one lunar month out of the year; and going to Mecca; and doing the tithe. These five pillars encompass your entire life. They fill up your days.

"To the Muslim, they are everything of who you are. When you give birth to a child, you whisper the creed into your child's ear. When you look at your finances, it has an Islamic stamp upon it. This is what we were taught and why it's so hard to reach out to Muslims. It is not merely *theological*. So many Christians dichotomize and divorce their faith from their life. In Islam you cannot do that."

Getting Personal—Worldviews in Collision

During the interview I noted, "In spite of all that you lived and practiced as a Muslim, you still both somehow became Christians. How did you come to think about Jesus Christ in a different way?"

In Ergun's words: "It was the tenacity of *one kid*—literally. The reason that Emir and I are in education is because of one high school guy in my life.

"You have to understand, we did not have contact with unbelievers. But after repeated attempts by my friend, I gave in and finally attended a church service with him. Immediately after the service, he took me to the pastor and said, 'Pastor, here's my Muslim friend.' The pastor asked me the question, 'Who is Jesus?'

"In Islam, this is a tough question. *Isa* ["Jesus" in Arabic] is one of the top twenty-five prophets. I replied, 'I respect *Isa* very much.' This is where he hammered down on me. He said, 'I run into a lot of people who respect Jesus, but that's not an option. What did Jesus do in the Qur'an regarding His crucifixion?'

"Inside I jumped. I said, 'Surah 4, verse 157 of the Qur'an says Jesus was not crucified. Somebody was crucified in His place.'

"He replied, 'That's right. But somebody *was crucified*. Why?' Crucifixion was for blasphemy. The point is, whether or not you believe Jesus was crucified, He was accused and indicted for blasphemy—claiming to be God."

While he was talking, I couldn't help but notice his logical predicament. In Mark 14, when Jesus was questioned after His arrest, He was asked, "Are you the Christ, the Son of the Blessed One?" Jesus replied with the simple but profound answer: "I am."

Ergun continued, "For us, this is profound. You try to explain the gospel to a Muslim, and you talk about the cross and Jesus shedding His blood and you think you're telling them something new. It's not! Muslims *believe* in atonement. We *believe* in atonement. We *believe* in blood! The difference is that we believe it is by shedding *our own* blood that we purchase our forgiveness. We believe *our* blood purchases our only eternal assurance. This is the concept of *jihad*—to die as a martyr in a declared *fatwa*. What we couldn't understand was that Christ died in our place.

"One of the great Islamic apologists, Shabir Ali, would always ask in debate, 'What would one man's death have to do with me?' The way the pastor reached me was that he explained that Jesus died on the cross so that I wouldn't have to. If I may be so crass, *Jesus strapped Himself to a cross so that I wouldn't have to strap a bomb to myself.*"

Family Feud

Emir then spoke about his family's history since their conversion. "We were disowned by our father. Our father wanted to somehow modernize a traditional verse from Bukhari's Hadith 9:57. It teaches, 'If a Muslim changes his Islamic religion, kill him.' In fact, it's stated again in 4:260. It is not only treason against the state; it is treason against Allah. It's traditional Islam."

Ergun leaned forward, confirming his brother's words. "We're now twenty-two years removed from this. When I went to my father and said, 'Baba, I believe Jesus Christ is the Son of God,' it marked me for death. I didn't know this at the time. I wanted him to know grace. I wanted my father to be liberated. I wanted my brothers and my mother to be liberated.

"Our father disowned us. I didn't see him for another seventeen years. I tell this in churches and people get teary-eyed. But for us, our father's actions were an act of mercy. In over thirty countries around the globe today you are put to death. On Friday, on *jumyaat* prayer, you are buried up to your waist in your burial cloth and stoned to death. In Pakistan it's called Rule 295-C: to blaspheme the Prophet Muhammad, meaning to convert to anything else. *Put to death.*"

Islam Around the World

At this point, I shared from a then-late-breaking story regarding the Afghanistan Supreme Court, asking the Caners for their comments as experts on this issue. The court had declared that a man who had converted to Christianity faced the death penalty because he refused to revert back to Islam.

Ergun disclosed a dark secret about Muslim society in America that I did not know. "Many Muslims who come to faith in Christ here in America have their parents fly them home for what we would affectionately call 're-education.' They are given two options. One, they must revert. The vast majority of them do revert if they are flown home. Second, you have to be declared insane in order to live, which is what the Afghan court tried to do. The problem is that any Islamic nation that calls itself an Islamic republic cannot allow freedom of conscience, freedom of thought, or freedom of conversion."

An Encouraging Word to Muslims

As we wrapped up the interview, I asked Emir what he would say to Muslims who desired to change but were still looking to their obedience and good works to outweigh their wrong acts. "If they want to place their faith in Christ, what would you suggest?"

Emir shared, "Picture being in a courtroom guilty of murder, trying to plead your case. As you're pleading your case you say, 'I feel like I'm a better man.' Your wife stands up, your boss stands up, your kids stand up, and they all say you're a good husband, good father, and a good employee. Then you turn to the judge and say, 'I deserve to be released, even though I'm a murderer.' That is what is said about the scales in chapter 23 of the Qur'an, that somehow the good can outweigh the bad.

"But biblically there must be justice for what you have done wrong. Only the atonement of Jesus Christ provides this solution. No other faith can. In the atonement of Jesus Christ you have a choice—you either pay for your own sins, according to Revelation 20, or the blood of Jesus Christ is poured out for your sins—past, present, and future. Christianity is the only religion in the world to do that."

Ergun and Emir's written words provide a fitting summary of these thoughts:

> The extent of the atonement is determined by the extent of God's love. Islam teaches that Allah's love and forgiveness is conditioned upon one's righteousness (Surah 2:279; 17:25; 19:60). The Bible teaches that God's love and forgiveness is unconditional, based not on how good one has been but on the death of Jesus. Jesus paid the infinite cost of sin on

behalf of those who accept that atonement for their own lives (Romans 10:9-10,13). Salvation is not founded upon the enduring work of each person but on the finished work of Christ (John 19:30). To maintain that Jesus Christ died for the world affects one's theology. To admit that Jesus Christ died for me affects my eternal destiny.[25]

In the next chapter, we'll discover how the traditional Muslim concept of jihad is influencing Islam today. Ergun and Emir will explain how the radical theology of jihad drives the conflict now taking place in the Middle East.

4

Islam's Extremes: Evaluating Jihad Today

*"My Muslim brothers of the world: Your brothers in
Palestine and in the land of the two Holy Places [Mecca and
Medina in Saudi Arabia] are calling upon your help and
asking you to take part in fighting against the enemy—your
enemy and their enemy—the Americans and the Israelis.
They are asking you to do whatever you can, with one
means and ability, to expel the enemy, humiliated and
defeated, out of the sanctities of Islam."*[26]

OSAMA BIN LADEN

*"The governments of the world should know that Islam
cannot be defeated. Islam will be victorious in all the countries of the world, and Islam and the teachings of the Koran
will prevail all over the world."*[27]

AYATOLLAH RUHOLLAH KHOMEINI

One of the most violent and extreme words in our world today
is *caliphate.* Do you know what the word means? In a riveting interview with the *Christian Science Monitor* a spokesman for the Muslim
organization *Hizb ut-Tahrir* defined it this way: "Muslims should
abolish national boundaries within the Islamic world and return to a
single Islamic state, known as 'the caliphate,' that would stretch from
Indonesia to Morocco and contain more than 1.5 billion people."[28]

Vice President Dick Cheney used this word in September 2004
when he referred to Osama bin Laden and his followers as "wanting
to re-establish what you could refer to as the seventh-century
caliphate to be governed by sharia law, the most rigid interpretation
of the Qur'an."[29]

General Abizaid, a top American commander in the Middle

A RELIGION OF PEACE?

On May 8, 2006, President Ahmadinejad of Iran sent a letter to U.S. president George W. Bush. He called on Bush to accept Islam, ending his letter by commenting, "...Mr. President, history tells us that repressive and cruel governments do not survive."

In a Hadith, Muhammad tells his followers to call people to Islam before waging war against them:

> Fight in the name of Allah and in the way of Allah. Fight against those who disbelieve in Allah. Make a holy war.... When you meet your enemies who are polytheists, invite them to three courses of action. If they respond to any one of these, you also accept it and withhold yourself from doing them any harm. Invite them to (accept) Islam; if they respond to you, accept it from them and desist from fighting against them.... If they refuse to accept Islam, demand from them the Jizya [the tax on non-Muslims specified in Qur'an 9:29]. If they agree to pay, accept it from them and hold off your hands. If they refuse to pay the tax, seek Allah's help and fight them (Sahih Muslim 4294).[33]

East, warned the House Armed Services Committee in September 2006 that "[Muslim radicals] will try to re-establish a caliphate throughout the entire Muslim world ...*the caliphate's goals would include the destruction of Israel*"[30] (emphasis added).

U.S. political leaders have also begun to notice these beliefs. On February 4, 2006, former Secretary of Defense Donald Rumsfeld pointed to the global nature of the caliphate, stating that radical Islam "seeks to take over governments from North Africa to Southeast Asia and to re-establish a caliphate they hope, one day, will include every continent. They have designed and distributed a map where national borders are erased and replaced by a global extremist Islamic empire."[31]

On February 28, 2006, John D. Negroponte, U.S. Director of National Intelligence, testified that the U.S. government knows that "Ayman al-Zawahiri, Al Qaeda's number two, is candid in his July 2005 letter...that the jihad in Iraq [is] a stepping stone in the march toward a global caliphate, with the focus on Egypt, Syria, Jordan, Lebanon, Saudi Arabia, the Gulf states, and Israel."[32]

These goals are ultimately promoted by teachings in the Qur'an and Hadith. It's why since 9/11 the first name of bin Laden, Osama, has been the number-one favored name for newborn male infants in a dozen or more Muslim countries. In some nations, seven out of ten baby boys are namesakes of the terrorist.[34]

Dr. Emir Caner revealed in a March 2006 interview on *The John Ankerberg Show* that "if you want to see where Islam is going, it's going toward a *purist slant.* They're going back to the seventh century. They're doing so on such a scale that sixty percent of all mosques built in the world are built by the Saudis and are instituting the teachings of the Wahhabis. If you want to see what the Islamic world is doing, don't believe what most secular universities teach—that somehow Islam is a religion of peace and tolerance, and that everything is in moderation.

> "CAIR [the Council on American-Islamic Relations] has filed numerous lawsuits against those who say things about Islam that it doesn't like—making for a chilling effect on those who speak the truth about religion. They have Saudi oil money behind them and finances are no issue at all to them. They essentially have infinite funds. They will shut up everyone. On the topic of Islam, free speech is dead."[35]
>
> —ROBERT SPENCER,
> *THE POLITICALLY
> INCORRECT GUIDE TO ISLAM*

Instead, look to see what the Wahhabis are doing, what the Saudis are doing, and what's going on across the world where now more than two dozen countries have accepted the Islamic republic, where Islam has been accepted as the official religion, within the last two dozen years. That's where Islam is going."

The Sixth Duty

There is a sixth religious duty often associated with the five pillars of Islam, although it is considered optional by some. This is the Muslim holy war or jihad. *Jihad* may be interpreted as internal (as a spiritual struggle) or external (defending Islam). When the situation warrants it, this duty requires Muslims to go to war to defend Islam against its enemies. Anyone who dies in a holy war is allegedly guaranteed eternal life in heaven and is considered a martyr for Islam.[36]

What is jihad? According to Dr. Bernard Hykel, associate professor of Middle Eastern and Islamic studies at New York University, "Jihadism comes with a whole apparatus of propaganda, a whole worldview, a set of ideas, and a way of indoctrinating these ideas into people. People don't blow themselves up just because they wake up one morning. They need preparation. They need to be inculcated with certain views and ideas, and jihadism is very good about that."[37]

All Muslim leaders agree that military jihad should be undertaken only to ward off an attack. But of course, that is precisely what Osama bin Laden says that the September 11 attacks were doing. In his World Islamic Front statement of February 23, 1998, he proclaimed a litany of American offenses and then declared:

> All these crimes and sins committed by the Americans are a clear declaration of war on Allah, his messenger, and Muslims. And *ulama* [our communities] have throughout Islamic history unanimously agreed that jihad is an individual duty if the enemy destroys the Muslim countries.... Nothing is more sacred than belief except repulsing an enemy who is attacking religion and life.[38]

Radical Islam Grows in America

This violent interpretation of jihad can be found not only in Arab nations but in America as well. According to Sheikh Abdul Aziz Oudeh, a leading figure in the Islamic Jihad movement who spoke at an ICP (Islamic Committee for Palestine) conference in Chicago, Illinois on December 28-31, 1990, "Now Allah is bringing the Jews back to Palestine in large groups from all over the world *to their big graveyard* where the promise will be realized upon them, and what was destined will be carried out."[39]

Although Christianity remains the world's largest religion, Islam is the fastest-growing religion.[40] According to a CAIR (Council on American-Islamic Relations) 2001 mosque report, the majority of the more than 1,200 existing mosques (87 percent) have been founded since 1970...the collective Muslim population has grown to between 6 and 7 million in North America.[41]

As a disclaimer, we must first note that Islam has an enormous variety of subgroupings, similar to Protestant denominations, meaning that *not all Muslims hate Americans or Israelis*. What are discussed here are the *motives* of those Muslims who affirm or use violence as an expression of their religion.

A key example of the spread of this kind of hatred comes from the Center for Religious Freedom, which released a 2005 report exposing the dissemination of hate propaganda in America by the government of Saudi Arabia. The 89-page report is based on a year-long study of over 200 original documents, all disseminated, published, or otherwise generated by the government of Saudi Arabia and collected from more than a dozen mosques in the United States.[42] While these practices have long been known globally, its occurrence within the United States received little attention until after 9/11.

Within worldwide Sunni Islam the followers of Saudi Arabia's extremist Wahhabi ideology are a distinct minority, yet they are significantly responsible for the spreading of hate ideology within the American mosque system. Among the key findings of the report are these:

- Various Saudi government publications gathered for this study, most of which are in Arabic, assert that *it is a religious obligation for Muslims to hate Christians and Jews* and warn against imitating, befriending, or helping them in any way, or taking part in their festivities and celebrations;

- The documents promote contempt for the United States because it is ruled by legislated civil law rather than by totalitarian Wahhabi-style Islamic law. *They condemn democracy as un-Islamic;*

- The documents stress that when Muslims are in the lands of the unbelievers, *they must behave as if on a mission behind enemy lines*. Regarding those who convert out of Islam, the Saudi Ministry of Islamic Affairs explicitly asserts they "should be killed."[43]

Remember, this is what the report concludes has been spread *within* America! The ideology promoted by radical Muslim movements outside of the United States was not even included in this study.

The Worldview "Out There"

After Pope Benedict XVI cited a medieval reference about Muslims in a speech in September 2006, the Muslim world showed outrage, prompting a heightened security alert at the Vatican due to protests and even death threats. These responses included those sent from over 1,000 Pakistani clerics and religious scholars at a meeting in eastern Pakistan who demanded the removal of the pope for making "insulting remarks" against Islam, and warned the West of severe consequences if it didn't change its stance regarding their religion.[44] The worldview "out there" has become increasingly hostile of those who hold opinions that differ from those of Muslims.

Anyone not convinced that religion truly fuels the conflicts between Middle Eastern nations should consider the following statement from Nina Shea, the director of the Center for Religious Freedom, concerning Pakistan's blasphemy law:

> The U.S. government considers Pakistan an ally in the war on terror but [its] blasphemy laws are a form of state-sponsored terror against its own people. The U.S. should immediately reconsider its plans to sell F-16s to Pakistan until these laws are repealed and those accused of blasphemy are released from prison. Religious freedom is a keystone American value and a fundamental human right under international law.[45]

As we see here, military sales of F-16s are being discussed as a bargaining chip in an attempt to change a country's *religious* laws! Yet these hostile theology practices are not limited only to government laws. The hatred is also promoted the other way around, with radical spiritual leaders shaping military and political moves through teachings given inside local mosques.

Radical Islam's mission is to bring the "true faith" to the whole of mankind. In pursuit of this goal, Islamic radicals and fundamentalists (Islamists) resort to a range of tactics, from education, propaganda, economic support, and spiritual guidance to political subversion, terror, and war. An analysis of the focus of the conflict shows that the Islamists' primary concern is to reshape the political reality within the Muslim world.[46]

A recent example of this can be found within the Hamas movement, historically thought to be a threat only to Israel. However, in a translation provided by the Middle East Media Research Institute, we find Hamas leader Khaled Mash'al speaking in a mosque in Damascus, Syria on February 3, 2006 with some harsh words for Americans:

> America will be defeated in Iraq.... Wherever the [Islamic] nation is targeted, its enemies will be defeated, Allah willing. The nation of Muhammad is gaining victory in Palestine. The nation of Muhammad is gaining victory in Iraq, and it will be victorious in all Arab and Muslim lands. Their multitudes will be defeated and turn their backs [and flee]. These fools will be defeated, the wheel of time will turn, and times of victory and glory will be upon our nation, and the West will be full of remorse, when it is too late.... We say to this West, which does not act reasonably, and does not learn its lessons: By Allah, you will be defeated. Israel will be defeated, and so will whoever supported or supports it. I say to the [U.S. and European countries]: Hurry up and apologize to our nation, because if you do not, you will regret it.[47]

How frequently these types of comments are made in Middle Eastern mosques is difficult to calculate. Based on personal interviews and research with those who have contacts at mosques within Middle Eastern nations, such comments seem to vary depending on local leadership and locale. The likely scenario, however, is that the number of everyday Muslims who hear political messages encouraging violence toward America is growing, and at an alarming rate.

When Religion Is Law

Dr. Paul Marshall, general editor of *Religious Freedom in the World*, noted the powerful connections between religion and national law in some Muslim nations that provide severe consequences to those who question Muslim beliefs. His words here deserve careful attention:

> Western attention to extreme sharia focuses on inhuman punishments, such as amputations or stoning to death

women accused of adultery, but its effects are far wider. *Its major threat is that it equates questioning the government or laws with questioning God,* so that political opposition is treated as apostasy or blasphemy. Hence, it directly negates political and religious freedom by criminalizing dissent and debate.

When Sima Samar was appointed as the only Afghan female cabinet minister, the chief justice, Fazul Shinwari, charged her with "blasphemy," which carries the death penalty. Her "crime" was allegedly telling a Canadian magazine she did not believe in sharia.

In Iran, all political activity is conditioned on "compatibility with standards of sharia." In July 2004, professor Hashem Aghajari was sentenced to five years in prison for "insulting Islamic values" when he criticized the government's version of Islam. Similar strictures fall on reformers in Saudi Arabia, Egypt, Nigeria, Sudan, Pakistan and Bangladesh.[48]

While Americans may find such practices harsh, the everyday reality is that in Syria, a person must be a Muslim to be president,[49] Saudi Arabia is one of ten countries in the world which does not have a modern constitution but has stated that its constitution is the Qur'an,[50] and at least 24 Muslim nations continue to execute those who dare to convert to another religion.[51]

It is also important to note that there are now more people attending mosques in Britain than the Church of England.[52] There are so many Muslims living in Britain now that there is talk of allowing Muslims to live under sharia law in their neighborhoods.[53] The growth in the number and influence of Muslims in Western nations should be an issue of major concern to government leaders.

How Should We Respond?

What can we do to respond appropriately to radical Muslim hatred? The Bible provides several principles for us to apply. Rusty Wright's article "Why Radical Muslims Hate You" provides several helpful applications.[54]

First, *love your enemies.* Jesus taught, "Love your enemies, and pray for those who persecute you."[55] It is not emotionally easy to love Osama bin Ladin or to pray for Iranian president Mahmoud Ahmadinejad. Yet this is the teaching of Jesus and of the Bible.

Second, *support national defense.* The apostle Paul wrote that governments are to "bear the sword"[56] to subjugate evil. "The implications are complex and debatable, but the principle of defending against attack is biblical."[57] As I (Dillon) recently heard on the *Sean Hannity Show,* the number-one thing armed forces personnel desire from Americans is their support.

Third, *learn about Islam.* Hopefully this book is one step in your learning journey. In the Jewish Scriptures, those who "understood the times" were considered of great value to the leaders of their day.[58] According to the New Testament, the missionary Paul also sought information regarding the religious views in the cultures he was attempting to influence.[59]

Finally, *befriend some Muslims,* possibly from your neighborhood, school campus, or workplace. Show genuine concern for their lives, background, and perspective. When the opportunity opens, share your story of faith regarding a relationship with Jesus—a relationship that moves beyond the rituals and religion. As you build into the lives of others, not only will you see change; you will in turn be changed as God uses you to impact the worldviews of Muslims.

5

Judaism's Importance:
Abraham Points the Way

*"The LORD had said to Abram, 'Leave your country, your
people and your father's household and go to the land
I will show you. I will make you into a great nation and I
will bless you; I will make your name great, and you will be
a blessing. I will bless those who bless you,
and whoever curses you I will curse; and all peoples on earth
will be blessed through you.'"*

GENESIS 12:1-3

Long before Christianity and Islam came on the scene, Judaism's journey began through the ancient narrative of Abram. Later known as Abraham, Genesis records his calling to a new land where God would bless him and make his name great.

The Jewish story continues through Isaac, Jacob, and Jacob's 12 sons, who became the leaders of Israel's 12 tribes. Then Moses freed Israel from Egyptian bondage, then came generations of judges and kings and times of conquest from outside nations. After the destruction of Jerusalem in A.D. 70, the Jewish people migrated to other nations around the world.

Yet in 1948 something transpired that transformed Jewish history—Israel again became a nation. Emerging from the horrific holocaust of World War II, the Jewish people were provided a home, a physical land where they could return en masse from around the world to reunite culturally and spiritually. The nation that began with less than 100,000 Jews now boasts a heavily Jewish population of nearly seven million people.

Why such controversy about Israel? Many factors converge,

leaving room for much interpretation and speculation among today's experts. In an interview with Jewish-Christian studies expert Dr. Jimmy DeYoung, I (John) asked some of the more pressing questions regarding the Jewish religion and its importance today.

The Importance of Israel

Dr. DeYoung first moved to Israel in 1991, only days before hearing the air sirens that warned of SCUD missiles heading toward the city in which he lived. Undeterred, he remained for well over a decade, interviewing every Israeli prime minister for the past 16 years as well as hundreds of other Arab and Israeli governmental, military, academic, and religious leaders.

Because of his broad range of experiences in the Jewish homeland, the first interview question[60] I posed to him was, "Having lived in Israel, what do you believe about the nation's importance in today's world?"

He quickly commented on a biblical understanding of the nation. "Israel is God's timepiece. We can understand exactly where God is in His prophetic scenario simply by looking at Israel. The key to understanding all of biblical prophecy is found in Daniel 9:24. He said, in effect, 'I have a special plan for a special people in a special place.' Those special people are the *Jewish* people. That special place is *Jerusalem*. As you focus on those two entities, the city of Jerusalem and the Jewish people, you will understand what God is doing in this time in which we're living, this time in which God is starting to bring this prophecy into fulfillment.

"In Ezekiel 37 God gave us the story of the valley of dry bones. He then explains what He was talking about when He was saying the bones are going to come together. The bones will have flesh on them and will be filled with the breath of life. Those bones are the whole house of Israel. They'll be gathered. And out of 108 nations of the world, they have been gathered.

"I've lived in Jerusalem since 1991. We've seen over one million Soviet Jews immigrate to the land of Israel. Jeremiah 16, 23, 31 and Zechariah 2 all said at the time of the end we'll not talk about the exodus out of Egypt anymore, but we'll talk about the exodus out of the north, in which God is gathering Jews from all the nations of the world."

Noting his work with other media agencies in Israel, Dr. DeYoung said, "As a journalist living in Jerusalem, I monitor other news-gathering organizations. On May 24, 1991, I was listening to the BBC. As I was listening, I heard somebody give a report about 'Operation Solomon.' I wasn't exactly sure what that was, but I got on the line to some of my unnamed sources and found out some of what was taking place. I made an educated guess and reported over a news network in the United States, beating ABC, NBC, CBS, and everyone else by about two-and-a-half hours.

"Forty-two aircraft took off on a Friday evening. In Israel, airplanes don't fly on Friday night. That's *sabbat,* the Sabbath. They took off and flew to Addis Ababa, Ethiopia. Meanwhile, one of the most unbeliev-able logistics situations I've ever seen in my life occurred—15,000 Ethiopian Jews were airlifted and transported to Israel in 24 hours!

"One 747 normally carries about 500 with people taking up every seat. They had 1,087 people on the airplane. While the flight was in the air from Addis Ababa, Ethiopia to Ben Gurion Airport in Israel, seven babies were born—*in the air.* As I saw this and my wife and I greeted these Ethiopian Jews making their way into the country, we were endeavoring to help feed them. They didn't know how to open a yogurt container or crack a boiled egg. We were *feeding* them. Tears started to come to my eyes as I thought about Zephaniah 3:10, where it seems to allude to the time of the end, when God will reach into Ethiopia and bring His prize back to His land, to Jerusalem. That's what we're seeing unfold right now in the city of Jerusalem and throughout all of Israel."

The Palestinian Conflict

I knew the next question I wanted to ask was a very sensitive one. Dr. DeYoung had interviewed every Israeli prime minister since 1991 and spent time across the table from Yasser Arafat, King Hussein, and even King Abdullah from Jordan, and I wanted to know his thoughts about the Palestinian conflict: "How strong is the senti-ment over Jerusalem among the Jews and the Palestinians?" Again

Dr. DeYoung provided a quick history lesson on the complexity of the issues involved that connected Jewish Scriptures to the contemporary situation:

"In December 1995 the United Nations had a resolution come to the floor to vote that Israel has absolutely no jurisdiction over the city of Jerusalem. There was only one nation that voted against that resolution, and, of course, that was Israel. Even the United States of America abstained. This issue is very controversial."

Approaching this issue from another angle, I asked, "Jimmy, you've been a journalist there since 1991. So tell me, what myths are the media presenting to the world about Israel?" One of the key ones, he said, is "that Israel is holding down the Palestinian people—that Israel is making the Palestinians live in the refugee camps. That's not true. It's the Palestinian leadership that's causing them to live in those camps.

"I have some dear Palestinian friends who have become very successful because Israel has tourism as its number-one industry. Israel has invited the Christians of the world to come visit the land of their forefathers. Of course, the Palestinians can reap the benefits from all this if they will cooperate. . . . I have one Palestinian friend who's a guide. He has a home in Jerusalem, a home in Amman, Jordan, and a home in Switzerland. He has made it very well. He is an example of what can happen. So that's one of the myths that the media is propagating upon the world—that the Palestinian people have been held down by the state of Israel. Israel is willing to assist the Palestinian people and develop their communities, to help them develop electrical systems, water systems, to put their schools together, to train the children up. But the Palestinian leadership says no."

Regarding how news is reported from Israel to the United States and Europe, DeYoung told me, "You know, I've gotten on an airplane out of Tel Aviv at Ben-Gurion Airport and flown back to the United States. There is a seven-hour difference between the East Coast of the United States and Israel. I would report a story in Israel, get on the plane, fly back to the United States, listen to the newscast here seven hours later, and hear a completely different story. That's one of the major problems. Every media outlet has an agenda. Well, I have an agenda too. One of the reasons I went to live in Israel as a journalist is to tell the truth about what's happening—and that's what we've endeavored to do. But you've got to know the source from which you're getting the information. That is key, especially for a Christian. I believe that we, as believers in Christ, need to understand the times in which we're living. I always say I report the political news because it is what's setting the stage for the prophetic to be fulfilled."

Dr. DeYoung has continued to provide amazing insights into the connecting points between Israel's contemporary political situation and the spiritual significance of what's happening. As political upheaval against Israel grows, the need for DeYoung's message, based on the messages of the prophets of old, will continue to spark interest and controversy for those desiring to better understand the nature of the Middle East meltdown.

6

Christianity's Origins: Jesus as *the* Way

*"Jesus answered, 'I am the way and the truth and the life.
No one comes to the Father except through me.'"*

JOHN 14:6

"In no other case is the interval of time between the composition of the books and the date of the earliest extant manuscripts so short as in that of the New Testament. The interval, then, between the dates of original composition and the earliest extant evidence becomes so small as to be in fact negligible.... Both the authenticity and the general integrity of the books of the New Testament may be regarded as finally established."[61]

DR. FREDERICK KENYON

On a warm winter night in a well-known Orlando, Florida hotel conference center, I (John) had the opportunity to gather eight well-known evangelical Christian scholars from various disciplines to provide insights on some of the top issues of today. What surprised me the most from that three-hour session of intense dialogue was not so much the kind of information shared, but the passion of those sharing the information. This helped my listening audience and I to walk away with an enhanced understanding of the beliefs we say are of greatest importance as followers of Christ.

The Reliability of the New Testament

One of the key questions of our day is, "Are the New Testament books reliable?" Do we really know what Jesus said and did? Some modern scholars, going back to F.C. Bauer and Rudolph Bultmann, said that the Gospels of the New Testament were written as many as 200 years after the time that Jesus lived—that we really don't have anything but legend and myth. Recent novels, accentuated by the controversial plotline of Dan Brown's international best-seller *The Da Vinci Code*,[62] have generated many thoughts and questions among readers eager to discover alternative theories regarding Christianity's origins. Following after *The Da Vinci Code* is an assorted array of nonfiction titles that have also become best-sellers all across North America, such as *Misquoting Jesus*,[63] *The Jesus Dynasty, The Jesus Papers*,[64] *What Jesus Meant*, and *The Gospel of Judas*.[65] Each book in some way proposes a view of Jesus and the New Testament quite contrary to those presented by the Gospels, or the first four books of the New Testament.

Can we trust what historic Christianity taught about Jesus and the New Testament? I wondered how the experts in our 1996 interview would respond to the challenges now being raised by some of the alternative theories. What I heard was more than I ever anticipated...

The Dates of the New Testament Documents

Dr. Walter Kaiser received his PhD from Brandeis University, and studied six ancient languages in retracing the development of the Bible's original text. I figured if anyone would know about the reliability and accuracy of the New Testament, he would. In his response, he methodically described that "the most controversial of the four Gospels is John. John is said to be too theological; too developed. It's too personal and too evangelistic. But look at John Ryland's Papyrus. There's a little scrap of paper about two-and-a-half inches by an inch-and-a-half with a text from John 18 found deep in Egypt that is now dated at approximately A.D. 125. This was so impressive that Dr. William Albright, then at Johns Hopkins, claimed, 'This cannot be a second- or third-century Christian Gospel in the Christian century. It must be the earliest of the Gospels.' So he dated John's Gospel A.D. 45. Now that's much more conservative than even me. I would be happy with A.D. 85–90. But he thought it was so impressive with its circulation so far deep into Egypt that he felt it was necessary to put it there. So I think there's very good evidence for going against the old hypothesis of F.C. Bauer and Bultmann and others [that the Gospels were written long after the lifetimes of the disciples].... The facts are hard to handle."

Dr. Robert Morey, author of more than 50 books, entered the discussion at this juncture. "I think we have to recognize that the well-known liberal Dr. John A.T. Robinson, who wrote the book *Honest to God,* which many college students were forced to read, later wrote a book entitled *Redating the New Testament,* in which he said all of the New Testament books were written before A.D. 70 and the destruction of the temple. He came to this conclusion on the basis of *internal* evidence. Here is a liberal who is more conservative now than most conservatives."

Offering a more bottom-line perspective, best-selling author Dave Hunt jumped in: "Keeping in mind the ordinary person who doesn't have all of these degrees, let's just read the Bible. John claims it was what he *saw,* what he *handled.* He and the other authors claimed to be either eyewitnesses or to have had contact with the eyewitnesses. Now, either these guys had the secret of longevity or they're liars. As you read the New Testament and the moral impact it has had on people's lives, you can't believe it was concocted by liars."

The Transmission of the New Testament

Clarifying our direction at this point, I refocused my question, seeking greater understanding regarding the New Testament's transmission through the years—plus I wanted to challenge these experts a little bit. Turning to Dr. Walter Kaiser, I asked, "Walter, when we examine the New Testament books, some people say, 'You know, it came through all those monks in the Middle Ages. Some of them were drunk, weren't too sharp, and made a lot of errors.' How do we know that the copies that we have today are really what Matthew, Mark, Luke, and John actually wrote?'"

Dr. Kaiser sat up in his chair and drew in a deep breath. He said, "We have the science of textual criticism, in which there are so many copies of the New Testament available, going back so close to the actual date they were written, that it has been possible to pinpoint the actual text. We're talking between 4,000 major manuscripts up to 25,000, if you're talking about portions of it. No other book has been so well attested. No series of events or historical event in all history has had as much documentation as the New Testament documents. They are extremely reliable."

Jesus as God

Pressing my guests even further, I dropped the big question I had been holding onto up to now. "Some are saying that if you were to accept the New Testament documents as being reliable, you will see that Jesus never claimed to be God. Tell us why that really disturbs you. Tell us why it's clear to you that Jesus made direct claims to be God."

Dr. Kaiser wasted no time in responding first. "Well, I still think the best text is John 10:30: 'I and the Father are one.' Also, John 14:9 tells us, 'Anyone who has seen me has seen the Father.' You can fight about that but if you do, you go against the audience that was there. They understood Jesus and picked up stones. They were going to kill Him because they thought, *He's blaspheming. He's claiming to be God.* Jesus did not say, 'Oh, wait a minute. That's not what I'm saying at all.' There's no record of that. He *did* claim to be God."

Joan Cetnar, a former Jehovah's Witness who had worked at the Watchtower headquarters in Brooklyn, New York, and later converted to Christianity, spoke up next. She has educated others for nearly 40 years on comparative religions and serves on the board of directors for Personal Freedom Outreach. She said, "When I finally got a correct translation of John 8:58, knowing who the 'I am' really is from Exodus 3:14-15 and Jesus' plain statement to the Jews in John 8:58, 'Before Abraham was born [or came into existence], I am!'— you just can't get away from that. But they [the Watchtower Society's leaders] tried. They tried real hard [they claimed Jesus was an angelic being, but not God]. It's just not correct. It doesn't stand up under any good scholarship, as my colleagues can testify."

Complementing Joan's thoughts was Dr. Anis Shorrosh, a native Arab Palestinian who had converted to Christianity. "Besides saving me, changing me, teaching me to love my enemies, giving me security for now and eternity, the last book of the Old Testament declares,

'And suddenly the Lord Himself will come to His temple,' Malachi 3:1. When Jesus appeared on the scene, He made the claims, 'I am the way and the truth and the life,' 'I am the light of the world,' 'I am the resurrection and the life,' and, 'I am.' The phrase 'I am' is equated with God's name. Most remarkable of all is John 1:1: 'In the beginning was the Word, and the Word was with God, and the Word was God.' He's *alive*. He's *real*."

Turning to Dave Hunt for his perspective, I asked, "In your studies, what have been the words that Jesus used that persuaded you He was God?"

"In John 8:31 Jesus said to those who believed on Him, 'If ye continue in my word, then are ye my disciples indeed; and ye shall know the truth, and the truth shall make you free' [KJV]. That must have set those Jews back on their heels real fast. 'Hey, I thought we were following the Word of God. Is He claiming to be God? Wait a minute. I thought we were Moses' disciples.' He's undoubtedly claiming to be God. You can't get away from it. In John 8:58 Jesus says, 'Before Abraham was, I am.' It was the straw that broke the camel's back. They were ready to kill Him at that point. You just can't deny it when you face the words of Jesus Himself."

Dave's words were quickly followed by those of my friend and researcher Dr. John Weldon. He recounted, "I was a skeptic right until my last year as an undergraduate. I really didn't believe in the Bible, didn't believe in God, and didn't believe in Jesus. Christ dramatically changed my life. I was amazed at the evidence for the truthfulness of Christianity. In John 5:22-23, Jesus said that all judgment had been given to Him and that men would honor Him even as they honor God. Now, no one can deny that the Father is honored as God. If men are to honor Jesus just as they honor the Father, then Jesus must also be God."

The Evidence for Christ as Messiah

Questioning Dr. Morey for further facts, I suggested, "Robert, a lot of people out there can make claims. It's one thing to establish the fact that Jesus claimed to be God. What evidence does Jesus offer to support that His claim of being God is true?"

Dr. Morey responded, "First there is the evidence of fulfilled prophecy. Isaiah 40 [written over 600 years before the earthly life of Jesus] said, 'Prepare ye the way' [KJV]. For who? For the Lord. For Yahweh. For God Himself—'the Lord…shall suddenly come to his temple' [KJV]. Regarding Bethlehem, He will be born there. His origins reach back to *olam,* into eternity, from everlasting to everlasting. Jesus, on the day He died, fulfilled 33 prophecies in one day—everything that happened to the very end fulfilled that He was, as was expected, the child [who] is born, the Son who is given, the mighty God, 'the *el Kabod*' (Isaiah 9:6)—it fulfilled prophecy.

"Second, there were the miracles He did. These proved He was God. Who else can raise the dead and do what He did? Then last, we are told in Romans 1 that God Himself declared to everyone who Jesus was by His resurrection from the dead. His resurrection was a resurrection to glory, a glorified body, immortal, incorruptible."

Because the resurrection is the most critical of Christian beliefs, I then asked, "What if someone says, 'I don't believe there was a resurrection'? What's the proof that Jesus rose from the dead?"

"First, for those who are familiar with the Scripture, the Bible teaches a *bodily* resurrection, not a ghost-like resurrection. Second, there's the physical reality. *There was no body in the tomb.* If the body of Jesus could have been found by someone, it would have been trotted out and there would have been trinkets and souvenirs. Third, there's the legal evidence. There is more evidence to convict Jesus of being alive than is necessary. Imagine if five hundred people gave testimony in court that John Ankerberg robbed one of the banks down here and said, 'I saw him.' Then along comes a skeptic who says, 'Well, five hundred people—they could have been imagining this. It was group hallucination.' That person wouldn't get anywhere. Jesus *ate.* He *drank.* He said, 'Touch. Feel. I'm not a ghost. This is real. This is the body that was on the cross. Here I am.' He *proved* it to them.

"When He made that meal at the shore, as Francis Schaeffer once told me, 'There were footprints in the sand.' *Footprints in the sand.* What else except the reality of the resurrection would change these pitiful cowards, these people who were depressed? They gave up on

Jesus. They went back to fishing. They went back to farming. They said, 'He's dead. He's gone.' The only ones who even cared were the women. Even they went on the third day to put perfume on Him because they thought He was still a corpse. Nobody would believe. They were not gullible people who were expecting a resurrection and got what they expected. They were forced, like Thomas, to acknowledge that Jesus was Lord and God by the *evidence*."

Making It Personal

Closing our time together, I asked Dave Hunt, "For people who want to come to know this Jesus who claimed to be God and proved it by coming forth from the dead on the third day, how do they come into a relationship with Him?"

"If He's alive, He's real. He's *God*. He can hear your prayer. You talk to Him. He said, 'I stand at the door, and knock' [KJV]. It's the door of every person's heart. He said this after He rose from the dead. 'If any man hears my voice and opens the door, I will come in and I will fellowship with him.'

"That's the way I came to Christ. I was bothered as a young fellow just before I went to high school. The summer before I started going to high school I said to a preacher, 'Suppose there's a secret doubt and I say I believe, but I don't really believe?' He said, 'Well, why don't you just leave it up to Jesus? If you open the door, He will come in. Why don't you just open the door and ask Him to come in and then leave it up to Him?' I did, and a transformation took place in my life. I know He's alive and I know He's God. *He changed me.*"

As I look back now, I realize more than ever how well Dave's words summarized the fundamental beliefs of Christianity: "I know He's alive and I know He's God. *He changed me.*" Christianity is much more than a religion. It is a relationship built upon both facts and faith, an equation Christians, even the most intellectual ones, reveal best through their living and not just their teaching.

Part 2

The Present: The Explosive Elements of the Meltdown

When the first Gulf War in Iraq began in 1991, I (John) gathered a panel of top Christian prophecy authorities for a conference about the Middle East. Within less than a week, over 5,000 people had registered, giving us a standing-room only crowd. Their responses hit mainstream media news worldwide, providing a greatly needed Christian response for those rattled by the nation's recent entry into the war.

Now, nearly two decades later, new battles have re-emerged, demanding yet another look at today's Middle East events. Though the number of nations and groups involved has increased, many of the same core issues remain.

First, we'll reflect on what is really driving the roller-coaster prices at the gas pumps—noting again the spiritual factors involved. Second, we'll investigate the theology of the radicals who are attacking the United States and other nations. And third, we'll observe how public opinion regarding the War on Terror both helps and hurts the process, providing some biblical guidelines for our responses to the government.

7

Oil: How *Fuel* Fuels the Conflict

"...there is no escaping that the region that has grabbed the greatest global attention during the past half century in matters of oil, the Middle East, remains critical for future energy supplies. In a way, all the scrambling to develop resources around the world today is intended to delay the day of reckoning. Although the Middle East produces a quarter of world oil supplies, it holds between two-thirds and three-quarters of all known oil reserves."[66]

SHIBLEY TELHAMI

A recent *Harper's Magazine* article by Bryan Urstadt graphically describes the doomsday possibilities of a major oil crisis:

> The economy will begin an endless contraction, a prelude to the "grid crash." Cars will revert to being a luxury item, isolating the suburban millions from food and gas. Industrial agriculture will wither, addicted as it is to natural gas for fertilizer and to crude oil for flying, shipping, and trucking its produce. International trade will halt, leaving the Wal-Marts empty. In the United States, Northern homes will be too expensive to heat and Southern homes will roast. Dirty alternatives such as coal and tar sands will act as a bellows to the furnace of global warming. In response to all of this, extreme political movements will form, and the world will devolve into a fight to control the last of the resources. Whom the wars do not kill starvation will. Man, if he survives, will do so in agrarian villages.[67]

In the fall of 2006, I (Dillon) filled up my minivan and paid $2.89 per gallon of gas. Three years ago, the same gallon of gas cost only

$1.85, more than a dollar less per gallon. And the prices continue to fluctuate, with some wild gyrations every now and then. For example, during the aftermath of Hurricane Katrina in 2005, prices spiked to as high as $5.87 per gallon in Stockbridge, Georgia, with prices of nearly five dollars per gallon spreading across the Southeast. Prices have since declined to more normal rates, but Americans continue to worry over gas prices today, especially in light of today's Middle East tensions.

Unfortunately, the near future shows little hope of steadying today's rollercoaster fuel prices. As *Bloomberg* journalist Brendan Murray writes, "Prices show no signs of abating in the last two-and-a-half years of Bush's presidency, with oil futures hovering near $72 a barrel through the November 2008 presidential election. That's creating a windfall for oil-producing nations that may thwart Bush's goal of promoting democracy and free markets from Asia to the Middle East and halting the spread of nuclear arms."[68] In total, America's foreign oil bill climbed 4.8 percent to an all-time high of $28.5 billion, reflecting record oil prices in July 2006, on pace to a whopping $776 billion in debt for the year.[69]

But what is *really* driving the prices at the pump? Experts offer various opinions, each revealing important connections to the War on Terror—connections resulting from the *religious tensions* in the nations involved.

Supply and Demand

Foundational to understanding today's oil prices is the dynamic of the supply and demand of oil. In recent years, the demand has become staggering. Analysts now believe that by 2010, world oil consumption may hit *95 million barrels a day.*[70] A recent *Boston Globe* article noted the harsh reality of the oil supply-demand situation:

> The worry is not that we'll soon run out of oil in an absolute sense.... The debate, instead, is over how many of those remaining barrels are recoverable.
>
> The peak, these analysts point out, is not a matter of total numbers, but the rate at which we can get the oil out of the

ground. *The world has very little surplus oil capacity today.*
Fed by unexpectedly high demand from India and China,
global consumption has grown briskly for the past several
years, and if production levels off, a gap will open up between
supply and demand. The result would be crippling shortages
and oil prices far higher than any we've seen. According to
Charles Maxwell, a widely respected oil industry analyst at
the brokerage house Weeden & Company, a 2 percent short-
fall can easily mean a 20 percent increase in price: "Everyone
around the world pays that huge penalty, in order to determine who's going to go without that 2 percent."

Maxwell himself thinks things will get pretty dire at that
point. A 20 percent spike, he says, "means that people can't
buy clothes and housing. It slows economic growth immea-
surably. And God save us from the time when instead of
going flat, production starts dropping off"[71] (emphasis
added).

Turning these statistics into meaningful data for the everyday
person is sometimes a difficult task. It's one thing to say that "sometime in 2006, mankind's thirst for oil will have crossed the milestone
of 86 million barrels per day, which translates to a staggering one
thousand barrels a second!"[72] It's another thing to note that the
world's oil supply chains are operating at an unbelievable 97.5 percent.[73] In other words, the current supply cannot be pushed much
higher than already available. That's why any seemingly obscure
problem, whether a pipeline shutdown or new concerns in Iran,
causes oil prices to bounce around wildly.

How is this relevant to religion? Simply put, many Arab countries
hate Israel, specifically due to religious conflict between Israel and
Islamic republics. Israel provides one of the only counterbalances to
the Middle East's stability; it is the main democratic government of
the region. As Senator James Inhofe of Oklahoma noted in a Senate
speech, "If Israeli Defense Forces were not able to bring peace to the
region, the United States of America would need to commit thousands of troops at the cost of billions of dollars to secure a land that
is critical to our national security inasmuch as the oil-rich Persian

Gulf is at stake."[74] In other words, the current conflict of Arab nations against Israel involves conflict on a *spiritual* level. This jeopardizes the current supply and demand greatly, with billions of dollars and the destiny of thousands (if not millions!) of lives affected as a result.

Developing Nations Increase Thirst

In addition to the fragile supply-and-demand situation in North America, the oil thirsts of nations experiencing rapid industrial growth are creating an additional demand that is driving the world oil market even further. When gas prices recently hovered above $3 a gallon in many places, analysts said the spike was due, in large part, to the rising demand in the 1.2 billion-strong nation of China, where economic growth was a whopping 9.9 percent last year.[75]

China, the world's largest country in population, has greatly accelerated its oil needs. As one source observes:

> China is not the biggest oil consumer in the world, that prize goes to America, nor is it the biggest importer—which is also the USA. What China outdoes the rest of the world at is the growth of its appetite. Ten years ago China imported no oil at all. Last year it overtook Japan to become the world's second biggest importer. Its thirst continues to grow. Imports are expected to rise another 40% this year. China's appetite for oil shows no sign of slowing. Today China has 10 million private cars—by 2020 that number will be 120 million.[76]

How is the demand for oil among nations such as China and India driven by religious beliefs? One only needs to note Iran's negotiations with China on a new major oil deal as an example. In an *Associated Press* report on February 17, 2006, it was reported that China Petrochemical Corporation signed a $100 *billion* deal to develop a major Iranian oil field. This may also help explain why China has been hesitant to support sanctions against Iran, making the War on Terror more difficult for America as it attempts to garner support for a halt to Iran's nuclear development capabilities. As one Reuters report put it, "Russia and China, with hefty business stakes in Iran, are resisting pressure for sanctions from fellow veto-holders on the Security Council, Britain, France and the United States."[77]

Iran has been developing strong oil-based ties with nations with growing fuel demands in order to stop U.N. sanctions and possible war. The same article notes Iran's prime minister speaking on nuclear development, saying, "Enrichment means production of nuclear fuel. We have passed the laboratory phase of this science and *by God's will* the next step will be industrial production" (emphasis added). Unfortunately, God's will, as this Iranian leader believes, includes spiritually motivated plans that could include major conflict against opposing nations, especially Israel and the United States.

Interestingly, during the 2006 U.N. sessions in New York City, Venezuelan leader Hugo Chavez attacked the American government and called the president "a devil." In another context he recently claimed that "if the United States attacks, we won't have any other alternative [but to] blow up our own oil fields. They aren't going to take that oil." These acts, along with Chavez's growing alliance with Iran's Ahmadinejad, continue to increase already-heightened oil price tensions.[78]

The Ongoing War on Terror

Recently, *U.S. News & World Report* stated that "the overwhelming judgment from a hundred foreign policy experts polled in *Foreign Policy* magazine is that the highest priority in fighting terrorism must be to reduce America's dependence on foreign oil."[79] The bottom line is that when the United States confronts terrorism, those lands harboring terrorists become very sensitive locations, especially regarding the export of oil.

In 2004, the top world oil exporters included sensitive nations such as Iran, Iraq, Kuwait, and Saudi Arabia in the top 15 nations.[80] Four of the top five nations with the greatest known oil reserves include Arab nations, totaling *613 billion barrels*. The fact Arab nations control such an enormous amount of oil has a significant impact on any decisions made in the War on Terror.[81]

Tensions with Iran

As one writer observed, "Iran can pursue her nuclear ambitions with impunity as she confidently holds the ever-important oil card."[82] Iran, the world's fourth-largest oil exporter, claims to be developing nuclear power for "peaceful" purposes, but has been unconvincing in its arguments.[83] And the fact Iran's leaders are driven by their religious beliefs makes the situation all the more delicate.

Important in terms of oil, however, is how Iran's political moves on the nuclear issue impact oil prices. For instance, a Fox News headline on August 21, 2006 declared, "Oil Back Near $72 on Iran Refusal to Suspend Uranium Enrichment."[84] What is striking is that this news item was not in the *world* news: It was the top headline in the *financial* news. Iran's nuclear policies are clearly influencing the prices all of us pay at the pump.

One major concern noted by Dr. Mark Hitchcock is the importance of the Strait of Hormuz to the world oil market.[85] Located between Iran and the United Arab Emirates, it is a narrow passageway with only two one-mile-wide channels for sea traffic at its narrowest point. The best estimates are that 15-16.5 million barrels of oil pass through this point each day, representing approximately 20 percent of the world's oil supply. If Iran chose to do so, it could shut down this strait using sea mines or torpedoes. Such a move would have a detrimental impact on the world oil market, sending prices soaring for an indefinite amount of time.

As this chapter has shown, oil is the black gold affecting many decisions when it comes to politics, finance, *and* religion. But if you were to ask what the driving factor is, what is *really* determining the politics and finances, the observant researcher can find that it is the *theology* of oil-producing and consuming nations that plays the major role. This is the focus of our next chapter.

8

Theology: The Beliefs Behind the Battles

"There is a new generation that is willing to fight America, and this is something that America cannot stop."[86]

PALESTINIAN SHEIKH KHALIL AL ALAMI,
OFFICIAL OF THE AL-AQSA MOSQUE

"It's no longer a cold war of Russia, this is a confessional war. This is not one of ideology, it's one of theology."[87]

DAVID BREESE,
DURING AN INTERVIEW ON *THE JOHN ANKERBERG SHOW*

The central tenet of this book is that *religion* is the driving factor behind the War on Terror and the Middle East conflict. Theology, the study of God, provides the thinking for the spiritual beliefs of a religion. In our context, this not only includes the theology of Christianity, but also the theological beliefs of Jews, Muslims, and the extremist movements within each major religion that are at the forefront of today's terrorism headlines. The Islamic extremist theology that motivates today's terrorist groups will be the focus of this section, and the apocalyptic views of Christians will be addressed in later chapters.

As I was writing this chapter, I (Dillon) read about the latest audiotape release allegedly from the Iraqi terrorist leader Abu Hamza al-Muhajer, who specifically urged his al-Qaeda followers to kill at least one American in the next two weeks using a sniper rifle, explosive, or "whatever the battle may require," according to an audiotape that aired on *Al-Jazeera*. Al-Muhajer, which means "the immigrant," is the pseudonym adopted by Abu Ayyub al-Masri, an Egyptian militant believed to be an expert at making car bombs.

The speaker continued, specifically stating, "I invite you not to drop your weapons, and don't let your souls or your enemies rest until each one of you kills at least one American within a period that does not exceed 15 days with a sniper's gunshot or incendiary devices or Molotov cocktail or a suicide car bomb." At another point in the 18-minute audiotape comes the statement, "Our enemy has united its sides against us, and isn't it time to unite, *you worshippers of God?*" (emphasis added).[88]

Interestingly, within 24 hours of this declaration, a new car bomb exploded in Kabul, Afghanistan, and new insurgent attacks across Baghdad killed at least 20 people and 24 bodies were found dumped in the capital city—killings that bore the hallmarks of sectarian violence.

In this chapter, we're going to focus on two major movements of theological beliefs at work in the Middle East: Iranian theological extremism (and its variations), and the jihadist beliefs of al-Qaeda and its related groups.

Iranian Theology

The primary leader for the emerging religious extremism within Iran is its prime minister Mahmoud Ahmadinejad. Taunting U.S. president George W. Bush directly, he called for a debate at the United Nations, calling the United States "the Great Satan." Dr. Joel Rosenberg clearly summarizes the theological factors in this action, stating:

> Ahmadinejad has been agitating for a direct confrontation with President Bush and the nation he calls the "Great Satan" for some time. He believes he was chosen by Allah to bring about the downfall of Judeo-Christian civilization, and to usher in the End of Days, and he is getting more brazen and more dangerous with each passing month. Last fall when Ahmadinejad spoke at the U.N., he concluded his speech by calling upon the arrival of the Islamic Messiah, known as the "Hidden Imam," or the "Twelfth Imam," or the "Mahdi." He prayed: "O mighty Lord, I pray to you to hasten the emergence of your last repository, the Promised One, that perfect

and pure human being, the One that will fill this world with justice and peace." Back in Iran, Ahmadinejad stunned a group of Islamic clerics by claiming that during his U.N. speech, he was "surrounded by a light until the end" and that "all of a sudden the atmosphere changed there, and for 27 or 28 minutes all the leaders [in the audience] did not blink; it's not an exaggeration, because I was looking. They were astonished, as if a hand held them there and made them sit. It had opened their eyes and ears for the message of the Islamic Republic."[89]

In addition to his influence within Iran, Ahmadinejad has exerted his authority toward several factions throughout the Middle East, most notably with the Hezbollah movement in southern Lebanon and Syria. One political journalist has noted, "Iran appreciates the activities in line with the unique resistance of Lebanon against Israel, while *backing it with its spiritual and ethic supports*"[90] (emphasis added). Notice the attention is not on financial or military support (though this has been argued as well), but a *spiritual* support in helping other acknowledged terrorist groups incite violence with Israel.

Iran's influence extends even beyond Islamic nations. The same article notes the nation's ongoing efforts to include Russia, China, and others in an alliance that would help oversee the current situation in the Middle East. It specifically states, "Iranian envoy calls for Russia's more active role in Middle East."[91] Some even believe the recent movement of Russian troops into Syria signifies a supporting role with Iran.[92]

Having described the importance of his views, another journalist has rightly observed that "Ahmadinejad's 'vision' at the United Nations could be dismissed as pure political posturing if it weren't for a string of similar statements and actions that clearly suggest he believes he is destined to bring about the return of the Shiite messiah."[93]

The mystical Twelfth Imam, who is venerated by many in Iran, allegedly disappeared as a child in A.D. 941. Shiite Muslims believe he will return and rule for seven years in perfect justice. In a November

16, 2005 speech in Tehran, Ahmadinejad said that the main mission of his government was to "pave the path for the glorious reappearance of Imam Mahdi (May God Hasten His Reappearance)."

The article goes on to note that reports in government media outlets from Tehran have quoted Ahmadinejad as having told regime officials that the Twelfth Imam will reappear in two years. That was too much for Iranian legislator Akbar Alami, who publicly questioned Ahmadinejad's judgment, saying that even Islam's holiest figures have never made such bold prophetic claims.

At the same time the Iranian president has made such statements, he has repeatedly vowed to pursue Iran's nuclear programs in open defiance of the International Atomic Energy Agency and European Union negotiators. "While many Shiite Muslims worship the 12th *imam,* a previously secret society of powerful clerics, now openly advising the new president, are transforming these messianic beliefs into government policies."[94]

Most recently in his 2006 U.N. address, Ahmadinejad drew attention for slamming President Bush and speaking against Israel. Equally disturbing were multiple spiritual references, including:

- "The Non-Aligned Movement, *the Organization of the Islamic Conference* and the African continent *should each have a representative as a permanent member of the Security Council, with veto privilege.*" (Here he asks for an Islamic Conference [caliphate?] leader to sit on the permanent member board of the United Nations, and that this member be granted veto power.)

- "The Almighty and Merciful God, who is the Creator of the Universe, is also its Lord and Ruler. *Justice is His command.*" (While this *sounds* good, remember that the one stating this has in mind a theological view of justice fitting of radical Islam, meaning the destruction of those who do not join Islam.)

- "Bestow upon humanity that thirsts for justice the perfect human being promised to all by You, and make us among his followers and among *those who strive for his return and his cause.*" (A reference to the return of the Twelfth Imam, similar to a comment in his 2005 U.N. speech.)[95]

Putting this Shiite version of the end times into perspective, *Washington Post* writer Charles Krauthammer explains:

> Like Judaism and Christianity, Shiite Islam has its own version of the messianic return—the reappearance of the Twelfth Imam. The more devout believers in Iran pray at the Jamkaran mosque, which houses a well from which, some believe, he will emerge.
>
> When Ahmadinejad unexpectedly won the presidential elections, he immediately gave $17 million of government funds to the shrine. Last month Ahmadinejad said publicly that the main mission of the Islamic Revolution is to pave the way for the reappearance of the Twelfth Imam.
>
> And as in some versions of fundamentalist Christianity, the second coming will be accompanied by the usual trials and tribulations, death and destruction. Iranian journalist Hossein Bastani reported Ahmadinejad saying in official meetings that the hidden imam will reappear in two years.[96]

What does this mean for those who live in America? Best-selling author and political analyst Dr. Joel Rosenberg shares an insider's perspective on what is taking place among our very own government officials:

> On Tuesday [September 5, 2006], I was in Atlanta where I had the privilege of speaking to several dozen military commanders, Homeland Security officials, and disaster preparedness experts about these very issues. *We specifically discussed the End Times beliefs of Iranian President Mahmoud Ahmadinejad* and the implications of such views for U.S. foreign, defense and homeland security policy. We talked about how Russia is helping Iran go nuclear and arming Iran with state-of-the-art weaponry, and why they might be doing so. We talked about Iran's alliance with Hezbollah and how the recent war against Israel was just a prelude of things to come.
>
> The first question that was asked when my presentation

was finished: How should the U.S. respond to a leader who believes it is his religious mission to bring about the end of days, and who is feverishly pursuing the arsenal and alliances needed to bring his apocalyptic vision to pass? That, indeed, is the central question of the hour. We discussed it at length and I encouraged these staffers to help the leaders they serve get up to speed quickly on the radical Shi'ite End Times theology (or, eschatology) held by Ahmadinejad and his inner circle. Only then will they fully appreciate how dangerous is the current crisis and how little time the U.S. has to make a decision of how to stop Iran from launching its genocidal plans.[97]

It seems there is no doubt that the conflicts in today's headlines are ultimately *spiritual* in nature!

Theological Factors within Al-Qaeda

Peter Bergen, one of the few Western journalists to have interviewed Osama bin Laden face-to-face, recorded the words of Abdel Bari Atwan, the editor of the Afghani *Al Quds al Arabi* newspaper. During the interview, Atwan said regarding bin Laden:

> Now he went a step further or maybe more than ten steps further. He wants to say, now I am an international figure; I'm not just a Saudi. I am aggrieved at Americans who are occupying Saudi Arabia who are desecrating the Holy Land. That's the most important message he wanted to say. *I didn't expect him to actually declare a war against the United States* (emphasis added).[98]

Though bin Laden felt betrayed by the Muslims who had failed to join him at the time, complaining, "Only a few remained steadfast," and that "the rest surrendered or fled before they encountered the enemy,"[99] his popularity has continued to grow among radicals. Today, there are approximately 1.5 billion Muslims in the world. Most scholars agree that approximately 10 to 16 percent hold to radical Islamic ideas. This is frightening because it means that as many as 150 million Muslims would agree to the types of beliefs and actions promoted by bin Laden.[100]

In evaluating the motives behind al-Qaeda and similar groups, theology cannot be overlooked as a key ingredient. Speaking of the impact of religious extremism fueling war, Martin and Susan J. Tolchin write,

> The real question is, are these wars geopolitical or religious in nature? Are these fights really over land and water, with religion as an excuse, as in many parts of the Middle East and Africa? Are leaders manipulating their people for political power in the name of religion? Is religion synonymous with culture, and are these battles fought among belief systems, with political power as the goal, as in the Sudan? Or are these battles a potpourri of all the above?[101]

Even those writing from a cultural perspective are now acknowledging the fact that religious belief is a major component and driving force of this violence.

What About Christian and Jewish Theology?

We've discussed the extremes of fascist Islam found within Iran and its allies as well as the theological beliefs behind al-Qaeda. What does Christian and Jewish theology teach regarding these issues? During the 2006 conflict between Hezbollah and Israel, CNN's *Paula Zahn Now* program highlighted how the battles connected with Christian foretelling of the end times. Her broadcast summarizes the public's perception of Christian theological beliefs:

> ZAHN: There is bloody fighting in Lebanon, and Israel has a lot of American evangelical Christians wondering whether it's a sign foretelling the end times. To those who aren't evangelical, that may sound a little bit out there, but according to a CNN Harris interactive poll back in 2002, almost 60 percent of Americans think that the end of the world, as predicted in the Bible's book of Revelation, will happen, and 17 percent believe it will happen during their lifetimes.
>
> Now, this belief goes back centuries. Countless times, some Christians interpreted calamities as signs that the world was about to end. Of course, the world went on and on and on. And tonight, faith and values correspondent Delia Gallagher

is here because the Mideast fighting has many preachers and followers saying that the end is near again. Welcome.

DELIA GALLAGHER (CNN faith and values correspondent): I know it sounds a little far-fetched, Paula, but the fact is I've talked to a lot of believers who say the events that we are seeing were talked about in the Bible and do suggest that perhaps *the end is imminent*[102] (emphasis added).

Both Jews and Christians believe in a coming Messiah who will rule the world. The major difference in the Christian worldview is that it does not hold to violence by Christians to usher in the end times. While the radical extremes within Iran, al-Qaeda, Hezbollah, Hamas, Islamic Jihad, and others use their beliefs to justify their violence, Christianity teaches a *love* for enemies. Perhaps this helps explain the humanitarian concerns of Western nations with a Christian cultural heritage, even if those countries are not led by devout Christians.

For instance, in response to the 2003 earthquake in Iran that killed over 30,000 people, U.S. aid included over $5.7 million dollars for food, medical, and transportation support.[103] And that was not an isolated incident. Each year, the United States spends multiple billions of government dollars, in addition to massive amounts of missionary and humanitarian aid given privately, to help those in need worldwide.[104] Much of this giving arises from a religious or historical pattern of giving to those in need, as taught in Christianity.

A second difference lies in the Christian attitude toward the end times. While the radical Islam described in this chapter urges the use of violence to help bring about the end of time, Christians are taught to live holy lives in thankful response to the gift of eternal life from Jesus Christ. Though military conflict is not avoided completely within Christian thinking, it is not encouraged to help bring about the end of the earth.

Now That You Know

Islam's founding prophet Muhammad once wrote, "The ink of the scholar is worth more than the blood of a martyr." We hope the information in this chapter has proven this saying true. Now that you can see that the major influencing factor behind today's conflicts arises from religious beliefs, you are more able to appreciate why theology *must* be understood. You may also have a greater appreciation for what our government and military leaders face as they continue working through this struggle—an issue we will tackle in the next chapter.

9

Public Opinion: How It Helps, How It Hurts

"Today, on the Internet as well as on our best college campuses, people—even professors—are speaking in ways that could have landed them in federal prison sixty years ago. But the logic of our time is to ignore such 'harmless' conduct."[105]

TONY BLANKLEY

Tony Blankley, the editorial page editor of *The Washington Times*, noted in his 2006 book *The West's Last Chance* the tarnished changes taking place in America in the area of free speech:

> Free speech, cherished as it had been since before our founding, was seen to have practical limits when the nation was threatened in war. Children could be compelled to pledge their allegiance, even if their religion forbade it, because national security required national unity. Americans were determined to teach their children to be loyal to America, for fear that disunity would yield national insecurity, and, perhaps, national defeat.
>
> And while Americans continued to be free to say almost anything they wanted, even during war, if they spoke in favor of violence against the government or of violently overthrowing the government, the American public and the Supreme Court were perfectly prepared to put them into prison.
>
> Today, on the Internet as well as on our best college campuses, people—even professors—are speaking in ways that could have landed them in federal prison sixty years ago. But the logic of our time is to ignore such "harmless" conduct.[106]

While Americans have long enjoyed the right of free speech, Blankley argues that in recent years this privilege has lacked the responsibility of previous generations. Why the tremendous outcry against our government's leadership? Three major frustrations drawing outcries today include concerns about future terrorist attacks, frustrations over the prolonged war in Iraq, and the failure to capture Osama bin Laden.

Concerns About More Terrorist Attacks

Approaching the fifth anniversary of the 9/11 attacks, a Harris Interactive Survey revealed that many American and British citizens continue to worry about new terrorist actions. When asked, "How likely do you think it is that there will be a major terrorist attack in this country in the next twelve months?" 62 percent of Americans and 64 percent of British respondents answered that they felt the chances were "very" or "somewhat" likely.[107]

In other words, according to this study, five years after 9/11, the majority of Americans feel at least *just as worried* about a new terrorist attack as they did shortly following the 9/11 attack itself.

There are several contributing factors to these widespread concerns. Security alerts at airports, the abundance of television news on terrorism, terrorist themes in today's films and shows, border patrol problems, and failures to update security procedures in many areas of the nation serve as strong visual reminders.

One of the top-selling novels of 2006 was *The Kite Runner* by Khaled Hosseini. In it, he portrays the immigrant experiences of a young man named Amir, who moves to Fresno, California, from Kabul, Afghanistan during the Afghan war. Chronicling the Arab-American perspective of the events leading to and transpiring from 9/11, Hosseini offers readers a graphic and stunning insight into what even many Arab Americans fear concerning today's terrorism. There have not been only five years of concern; there have been a lifetime of worries.

With such concerns at stake, politicians have sometimes used these fears to point fingers and help form public opinion. For instance, in *The One Percent Doctrine*, Ron Suskind shows how "[John] Kerry had gained some ground in July by saying he would embrace all the recommendations of the 9/11 Commission. He criticized [only one person] Bush—rather than Tenet and the CIA—for intelligence failures, and challenged the President to fully accept, as well, the recommendations of the commission."[108] Certainly more than one person would have to be responsible for any mistakes made in the sweeping investigation of 9/11. Suskind notes that Kerry, among others, has used such controversies to help form public opinion.

Frustrations over the War in Iraq

Because the war in Iraq has been an ongoing endeavor rather than a short-term commitment, it has become the number one issue for our government to discuss, according to a recent poll.[109] Military families, separated from loved ones serving overseas, the economic impact, and the increasing number of lost lives are fueling a growing public backlash.

These frustrations have been vocalized during some of President Bush's recent speeches. One of the major protests occurred in Salt Lake City, Utah, where a crowd of thousands cheered Salt Lake City mayor Rocky Anderson for calling President Bush a "dishonest, war-mongering, human-rights violating president" whose time in office would "rank as the worst presidency our nation has ever had to endure."

With their signs labeling Bush, Secretary of State Condoleezza Rice, and former Secretary of Defense Donald Rumsfeld the "axis of evil" and calling the Iraq war a "mission of lies," the estimated 1,500 to 4,000 protesters hoped their demonstration at the Salt Lake City county building sent a message about the politically reddest state in the country. For those who didn't get enough during the daytime protest, organizers held a "Rock Against Rumsfeld" concert at Pioneer Park in the evening.[110]

Today's writers have also contributed to popular thinking about the war through their published criticisms. For example, in *Fiasco: The American Military Adventure in Iraq,* author Thomas Ricks makes comments such as, "[The War in Iraq] was made possible only through the intellectual acrobatics of simultaneously 'worst-casing' the threat presented by Iraq while 'best-casing' the subsequent cost and difficulty of occupying the country."[111]

The Failure to Capture Osama bin Laden

A third major factor influencing public opinion has been the failure (at least at the time of this writing) to capture Osama bin Laden. CNN's "In the Footsteps of bin Laden" chronicled the journey of this seemingly uncatchable character, revealing both weaknesses in the hunt and possible scenarios of an upcoming arrest. Despite a renewed senate approval of $200 million dollars to fund a CIA unit specifically designated to find bin Laden,[112] along with President Bush's comments that "it is just a matter of time,"[113] the results have been lacking. Ongoing controversies with Pakistan regarding its pursuit of bin Laden and Pakistan's law against outside military occupation have also complicated the situation.[114]

This failure has resulted in a tremendous lack of confidence toward some government leaders, and this has been further aggravated by high-level intelligence officials who have spoken out against the war effort. Ex-CIA agent Michael Scheuer is the senior intelligence analyst who created and advised a secret CIA unit for tracking and eliminating bin Laden in 1996. In November 2004, he spoke on the CBS program *60 Minutes,* and shared several negative views on the failure to capture or kill Osama bin Laden, thus causing another round of public uproar. He specifically blamed September 11 on poor leadership from people such as former CIA director George Tenet, his chief deputy, Jim Pavitt, and former White House counterterrorism czar Richard Clarke.[115]

How Should Christians Respond?

Following a speech in which Venezuelan president Hugo Chavez ripped President George W. Bush, U.S. Representative Charles Rangel was the first to speak out in support of Bush. His remarks included, "It should be clear to all heads of government that criticism of Bush Administration policies, either domestic or foreign, does not entitle them to attack the President personally."[116] One surprising aspect of this story was that the first official response came from a Democrat rather than someone from Bush's own Republican party. Why? The issue was larger than a political party; it was a matter of principle.

Amidst the controversies surrounding public opinion on the War on Terror, how should Christians respond? In Romans 13, the apostle Paul provides the foundational New Testament principle for respecting governing authorities:

> Everyone must submit himself to the governing authorities, for there is no authority except that which God has established. The authorities that exist have been established by God. Consequently, he who rebels against the authority is rebelling against what God has instituted, and those who do so will bring judgment on themselves.... Therefore, it is necessary to submit to the authorities, not only because of possible punishment but also because of conscience.[117]

Four specific insights emerge from these words. *First, Christians should respect (and submit to) governing leaders.* This could include refraining from speaking poorly in public of our nation's president and other leadership, along with obedience to government laws and regulations.

Second, God judges those who rebel. While the form of this judgment is not specified, it is clear that the results will be negative upon those who choose to not respect governing leadership.

Third, properly respecting our civil leaders is a matter of conscience. Rather than an opinion, this teaching is a spiritual directive from the Bible. Christians are *commanded* to respect civil leaders out of spiritual duty and conviction.

Fourth, the implication of these words is that Christians are involved in government. They can vote for or against people and policies, but are to do so respectfully. America's founders practiced this principle, setting an example for others to follow today.

Ultimately, America's leaders declare principles that continue to call for freedom and a concern for the well-being of all people. This is a message all U.S. citizens should continue to support. One of President Bush's speeches about the War on Terror provides a fitting perspective for all who seek an end to the ongoing war:

Like the struggles of the last century, today's war on terror is, above all, a struggle for freedom and liberty. The adversaries are different, but the stakes in this war are the same. We're fighting for our way of life and our ability to live in freedom. We're fighting for the cause of humanity against those who seek to impose the darkness of tyranny and terror upon the entire world. And we're fighting for a peaceful future for our children and our grandchildren. May God bless you all.[118]

Part 3

The Future: Where Is This Meltdown Headed?

"I've been watching the news from the Middle East full time.... I think that history began there, and it is going to end there. The whole Bible is centered in the Middle East and so many of the events that are taking place in some ways already have taken place many times, and my heart goes out to all those people who are suffering on all sides.... I pray for those people constantly—they're on my mind, they're on my heart. I pray that somehow they will find a solution. I'm not sure they will ever find a permanent solution. Christ, who I believe is going to come back, will settle all of those things in a great period of righteousness."[119]

Dr. Billy Graham, *Newsweek*, August 14, 2006

"The rise of terrorism in our world and the emerging crisis in the Middle East between Israel and Iran are part of a much bigger picture—that of God's plan for the future of Israel and the entire world."[120]

John Hagee in *Jerusalem Countdown*

When I (John) was growing up, I remember thoughts about sirens going off and nuclear bombs destroying American cities. Those fearful feelings of helplessness resurfaced as I watched the film *Flight 93*, which tells the story of one of the planes hijacked on 9/11. In the film are gripping scenes of the men and women on board as they call loved ones from cell phones in the moments before their tragic death. As the *9/11 Commission Report* notes, perhaps the greatest failure in preventing the deaths of the people on Flight 93 and 3,000 others on September 11, 2001 was not a lack of *intelligence,* but a lack of *imagination.*

Today's acts of sacred terror cause us to question what tomorrow holds. Is the end of the world near? Can we sleep without nightmares of another attack? Is there any hope for the future? In this section, we'll consider a panoramic view of how today's powers are "acting out" what the Bible portrays regarding the end times, confirming our hope that Bible prophecy is trustworthy both in its promise of judgment *and* its assurance of Christ's return.

10

Jerusalem in the Crossfire

"The Muslims say to Britain, to France, and to all the infidel nations that Jerusalem is Arab. We shall not respect anyone else's wishes regarding her."[121]

SHEIKH EKRIMA SABRI, PALESTINIAN MUFTI OF JERUSALEM
AT THE AL-AQSA MOSQUE, JULY 11, 1997

"Anyone who expects the Jewish state to make a peace that will redivide Jerusalem is not envisioning the kind of peace that we all believe in and think we can achieve."[122]

FORMER ISRAELI PRIME MINISTER BENJAMIN NETANYAHU

The above quotes quickly summarize the contrasting views of those battling over the city of Jerusalem. In the early 1990s, I (John) taped several television programs in Jerusalem on the life of Christ. My wife, Darlene, and I were invited by friends to visit a new diamond factory in the area. Once the owners found out we were with the media, they invited us to an area not open to the public. We walked down some stairs and found ourselves peering at several large religious bathing areas, along with a number of elaborate utensils.

I asked what these things were, expecting that they were for use in his diamond business. It shocked me to discover that the baths were designed to enable his workers to be ritually clean in order to serve the Messiah in the new temple. The tools from his basement were actually intended for use within the future Jewish temple!

He then showed me a framed poster that was a reprint of a local *El Al* magazine ad. It featured an aerial view of Jerusalem with one alteration in it: At the spot where the Dome of the Rock currently rests was an enormous Jewish temple. The Dome of the Rock was gone.

He told me that the area's Muslims were so upset by the ad that his business received several angry calls. The ad caused so much controversy that the issue even came to the attention of the Knesset, Israel's governing assembly.

During another taping in Jerusalem we met a Jewish couple who had moved there from Vermont. The husband was a masterful carpenter who could build anything out of wood. His wife, while reading the Old Testament, felt she had discovered the necessary dimensions for the Davidic harp and asked her husband to make one. We recorded her playing different harps that day, listening to the rich, melodic tones of the instruments. The sounds could have truly been the same as those made with harps in the time of King David.

Shortly after the harp's creation, a leading rabbi visited the couple to see the harp in action. When he touched it, he held it tightly to his chest with tears in his eyes. The wife asked, "Rabbi, why are you crying?" He answered that a rabbinic text had declared that when the harp returns to Israel, the temple would be near.

There are now thousands of trained Levitical priests, a reformed Sanhedrin, and a training school for temple worship training in Israel.[123] Israeli scientists have even claimed to identify the chromosome that identifies Levitical tribe members. A gold menorah for the temple, made from 100 pounds of gold, is now ready for the temple.

In a television interview in 1996, Dr. Renald Showers mentioned that "in Paris, France right now there's an elderly Jewish woman, a professional musician, who through extensive research, has rediscovered the exact kind of music that was played and sung in the temple worship services of Solomon's Temple and Herod's Temple. She has already set the Song of Solomon and the book of Ecclesiastes to that music. She's presently setting all 150 of the psalms to that music as well." Dr. Showers concluded his documentation of factors pointing toward the fulfillment of biblical prophecy by stating, "There are serious preparations for a new temple and God says it's going to be there."[124]

The Jerusalem Controversy

What is going to happen with Jerusalem, the ancient capital city that rests on the most controversial piece of land on the planet?

Research professor Dr. Renald Showers, who has taught for more than 35 years at some of today's top evangelical universities, said, "Historically, Jerusalem has been the capital. That's where the temples were located: Solomon's Temple and the second temple which Herod enlarged around the time of Christ. It has not only served as the *political* capital for the people of Israel, but it has also served as the *spiritual* capital for them.

"The prophetic Scriptures indicate that in the future Millennium the city of Jerusalem will once again be the capital city of not only the nation of Israel, but of the entire world. You have Isaiah, Micah, and other prophets indicating that during the Millennium it will be the spiritual and political capital of the world. That's where the Messiah will rule as King over the whole earth. Also, during the Millennium, all the nations of the world will come there to worship the Lord and to receive His instruction on how they are to live. Zechariah 8 says during that time, ten Gentiles will grab hold of one Jew and say, 'Take us with you up to Jerusalem to worship the Lord.'"

Dr. Showers's third comment startled me as he touched upon the politics behind modern Jerusalem. "There's a movement by our [U.S.] government as well as the United Nations and other nations to try to completely *internationalize* the city of Jerusalem and not let one nation control it but the world. Ever since the end of World War II up until only the past few years, the Vatican refused to recognize Israel officially as an independent government. Then when the Vatican heard there was a movement among the nations to take Jerusalem away from the control of Israel and internationalize it, the Vatican very quickly recognized Israel as a nation-state so that they could have, in essence, an embassy there. Their idea was if the world is going to determine what is done with this city, we want a voice in it."

The Samson Option?

During preparation for an interview on Jerusalem, I (John) stumbled across a book titled *The Samson Option: Israel's Nuclear Arsenal and American Foreign Policy.*[125] The author, Seymour M. Hersh, is a Pulitzer Prize winner, has written for the *New York Times,* and has won 12 major journalistic prizes. As I flipped through the book's pages, I couldn't put it down.

The book talks about the development of nuclear weapons by Israel. This development is called the Samson Option. Why? Samson was one of the early leaders of Israel who, because of sin, lost his great strength. But at the end of his life, God granted him strength for one last heroic act. Samson pushed down the pillars of the temple in which he stood at the moment, taking many of his enemies with him in death. [126]

I (Dillon) first discovered the concept of the Samson Option in a novel. I thought it had been made up. I later discovered the brutal reality behind the concept. During the first three days of the 1973 Yom Kippur War, Syria had invaded Israel from the Golan Heights and had broken through. Egypt entered from the south, making two enemies pressing from two directions. Prime Minister Golda Meir's cabinet met all through the night and concluded that the end had come. She decided to arm what they had recently code-named the Samson Option. If Israel was overrun, the nation would go down with its nuclear weapons. They allowed American and Russian satellites, according to Hersh, to see the silos where the nuclear weapons were uncovered so this information could be relayed to the Arab world. Russia actually told Egypt that "they had three nuclear bombs ready and to pull back."[127]

The Center of Everything

In my (Dillon's) conversations with John on the future of Israel, he mentioned some of the foundational beliefs the Bible presents on the issue. In his words, "Jerusalem is center of God's prophetic plan." God has chosen this city as His own. Jesus was crucified there, resurrected there, and will return and rule from there.

In an August 2006 blogpost, Dr. Joel Rosenberg mentioned the continuing significance of Jerusalem: "In more than 70 media interviews in the last three weeks, I've been trying to explain to people that this war [the Israeli-Hezbollah conflict]—at its core—is a battle for control of Jerusalem and the Temple Mount."[128] Daniel Pipes, a PhD graduate in Middle Eastern Studies from Harvard

University, notes theology's importance in the battle of Jerusalem, stating, "The debate matters. In Jerusalem, the theological and historical arguments matter, serving often as the functional equivalent of legal claims. The strength of these arguments will ultimately help determine who governs the city."[129]

Why Jerusalem?

Why is God allowing this? What is God's ultimate purpose? I (John) have friends in Jerusalem who have fought and witnessed their friends and relatives dying in war. They fought to defeat their enemies, who have outnumbered them as much as forty to one. Yet today leaders in Israel are willing to negotiate and give up the very land they have fought so hard to protect. Why?

After Israel's attack, Israel was besieged with protests. The prime minister defended the operation and vowed that Israel was ready to strike again, if necessary, to prevent any enemy from developing nuclear weapons. "If the nuclear reactor had not been destroyed," Begin said, "another Holocaust would have happened in the history of the Jewish people. There will never be another Holocaust.... Never again! Never again!"

FROM SEYMOUR M. HERSH, *THE SAMSON OPTION* (NEW YORK: RANDOM HOUSE, 1991), P. 10.

Veteran soldiers have confided to me, "My father fought so that I wouldn't have to fight. Then I fought so that my son wouldn't have to fight. Now my son is fighting so his sons and grandsons won't have to fight." Today's leaders are willing to give up the little land they have in the hopes they can finally live in peace. They are tired of fighting.

Today, if the United States were to back out as an ally to Israel, who would defend the country? According to the Bible, a future world leader will broker a seven-year peace deal, fulfilling Israel's longing for peace. But Scripture also says this peace plan will be broken, and Israel will be attacked once again. Countless armies will amass against them, with no human hope of victory. Only Christ's return, judgment, and reign will finally bring true peace in the Middle East.

In the meantime, several movements continue to cause conflict in the Middle East, particularly toward Israel, as God's eternal plan unfolds before our eyes. Our next chapter introduces the opposing force in Israel's most recent conflict, a conflict from the north that continues to set the stage for future controversies.

11

The Hezbollah Movement in Lebanon

*"The conflict has killed over 1,500 people, mostly Lebanese
civilians, severely damaged Lebanese infrastructure,
displaced about one million Lebanese and
500,000 Israelis, and disrupted normal life across all of
Lebanon and northern Israel."*[130]

On July 12, 2006, Israel and Lebanese Hezbollah forces began a conflict of remarkable proportions and captured the attention of the world for the next several weeks. Israeli prime minister Ehud Olmert said that "the war [had been] started not only by [the Hezbollah] killing eight Israeli soldiers and abducting two, but by shooting Katyusha and other rockets on the northern cities of Israel on that same morning—*indiscriminately.*"[131] In the process, over 1,500 people were killed and ten times that many people displaced in what has become a critical humanitarian situation. A U.N.-brokered cease-fire took effect a month later on August 14, and though the conflict was brief, it exposed a major religiously motivated dilemma that had been brewing for many years.

The average American has little information regarding the beliefs of Hezbollah. Who are they? What do they believe? Where are their loyalties? What we find as we peek into the world of the Hezbollah is a mix of political and spiritual motivations driving a reckless out-pouring of violence toward the nation of Israel.

Who Are the Hezbollah?

The Council on Foreign Relations provides perhaps the best definition of the Hezbollah movement when it states, "Hezbollah is a Lebanese umbrella organization of radical Islamic Shiite groups and organizations. It opposes the West, seeks to create a Muslim fundamentalist state modeled on Iran, and is a bitter foe of Israel. Hezbollah, whose name means 'party of God,' is a terrorist group believed responsible for nearly 200 attacks since 1982 that have killed more than 800 people, according to the Terrorism Knowledge Base."[132]

Experts note that Hezbollah is also a significant force in Lebanon's politics and a major provider of social services, schools, hospitals, and agricultural services for thousands of Lebanese Shiites. It also operates the al-Manar satellite television channel and broadcast station.[133]

How Did Hezbollah Begin?

Hezbollah was founded in 1982 in response to the Israeli invasion of Lebanon during the Lebanon War. Its official charter began on February 16, 1985, merging a coalition of groups known as Islamic Jihad. Though some argue whether this is the exact date, most scholars agree that the charter, discussed below, provides the historic beginning point for the movement.

What Do the Hezbollah Believe?

Hezbollah's charter document, *The Hizbollah Program,* clearly defines the three main objectives of its movement:

> The sons of our *umma* [community] are now in a state of growing confrontation with them, and will remain so until the realization of the following three objectives:
>
> - to expel the Americans, the French and their allies definitely from Lebanon, putting an end to any colonialist entity on our land;
>
> - to submit the Phalanges [enemy armies] to a just power and bring them all to justice for the crimes they have perpetrated against Muslims and Christians;
>
> - to permit all the sons of our people to determine their

future and to choose in all the liberty the form of government they desire. We call upon all of them to pick the option of Islamic government which, alone, is capable of guaranteeing justice and liberty for all. Only an Islamic regime can stop any further tentative attempts of imperialistic infiltration into our country.[134]

In another part of the charter, we see a further definition of these beliefs:

We see in Israel the vanguard of the United States in our Islamic world. It is the hated enemy that must be fought until the hated ones get what they deserve. This enemy is the greatest danger to our future generations and to the destiny of our lands, particularly as it glorifies the ideas of settlement and expansion, initiated in Palestine, and yearning outward to the extension of the Great Israel, from the Euphrates to the Nile.[135]

Why this intense hatred of Israel and the United States? According to Hezbollah, they believe Israel has occupied lands that belong to them. Again, this is a *spiritual* issue as it often focuses on Jerusalem, the holy city of Israel as well as the third most holy city in Islam. The conflict over the Temple Mount, now occupied by the Muslim Dome of the Rock, stands as a major controversy. Further disputes continue for other areas of Israel's land.[136]

According to the Institute for Counter-Terrorism, "The ideological basis of Hizballah is Khomeinism and its principle goal is the establishment of a pan-Islamic republic headed by *religious clerics*"[137] (emphasis added). In other words, Hezbollah seeks a nation led by Islamic religious leaders, and its proponents have been resorting to violence in order to obtain it. That *spiritual* motivations are at the core of this movement should be clear to anyone aware of Hezbollah's objectives.

Hezbollah Connections

"What a lot of people want to do is just say, 'OK, cease fire,'" President George W. Bush told Newsweek's

Richard Wolffe onboard Air Force One early last week.
"But you haven't really addressed the underlying cause
of the problem"—meaning the power of Hizbullah and
it backers in Iran and Syria.[138]

Hezbollah has recently been the focus of much attention due to its relationships to both Syria and Iran, in addition to several alleged connections with terrorist groups.

Syria. It is widely believed that Hafez al-Assad, who was president of Syria from 1971 to 2000, and Hezbollah were closely linked. This did not, at the time, significantly affect his relations with the rest of the world. Bashar al-Assad, his son and successor, has been subjected to sanctions by the United States due to (among other things, such as occupying Lebanon) his continued support for Hezbollah, which it views as a terrorist organization.[139]

Recently Syria has shown frustration at U.N. attempts to stop Hezbollah, including the suggestion of an alternative cease-fire.[140] Despite declaring efforts to impose an arms embargo against Lebanese Hezbollah,[141] at the time of this writing, Syria's leadership continues to warn against U.N. troops guarding the Syrian-Lebanese border, "saying such a move would be 'hostile' to Syria and create problems between the two nations."[142]

Christian researcher and author Gary Kah notes the significance a military conflict in Syria could cause on a larger scale, stating, "Attacking Syria would be like attacking Russia, especially since Russia still has thousands of military advisors, strategists, and Special Forces in that country.... Nevertheless, in order to stamp out terrorism, America will have no choice but to deal with Syria at some point. Why? Syria either supports or is home to more terrorist organizations than any other Islamic state."[143]

Clearly, Syria stands as a critical point of tension in the sacred terror of our day. For the international community to upset Syria could spark tremendous problems in the days ahead.

Iran. The *Los Angeles Times* reported that "Iran's relationship with Lebanon's Shiites is a complex web stretching back decades and spanning nearly all facets of religious, economic and social life—ties that have grown stronger since hard-line Iranian President Mahmoud Ahmadinejad came to power last year."[144]

An April 2002 BBC documentary provides a well-developed story for the historic and current connection between Iran and Hezbollah.[145] Their common cause? A desire to destroy Israel. Why? Once again there is a *spiritual* motivation. On August 3, 2006, Iranian president Mahmoud Ahmadinejad said the solution to the Middle East crisis is to "destroy Israel." He continued his speech by claiming that Israel "is an illegitimate regime, there is no legal basis for its existence."[146] He argues that Israel's land "belongs" to Muslims rather than to Jews, a view deeply rooted in Ahmadinejad's Islamic beliefs.

According to *Time* magazine, "There isn't the slightest degree of ambiguity or doubt as to Iran's role in this [war]," says a French foreign-affairs official. "How much coincidence could there be in Hizbollah kidnapping the Israeli soldiers on the same date that ministers met in Paris to decide what measures to take on the Iranian nuclear issue? None, in our opinion."[147]

Hamas. A Congressional Research Services report for the U.S. Congress had this to say:

> Although Hezbollah and Hamas are not organizationally linked, Hezbollah provides military training as well as financial and moral support to the Palestinian group and has acted in some ways as a mentor or role model for Hamas, which has sought to emulate the Lebanese group's political and media success. Hamas's kidnapping of the Israeli soldier follows a different Hezbollah example. Moreover, these two groups share the goal of driving Israel from occupied territories and ultimately eliminating it; *both maintain close ties with Iran*.[148]

According to an Israeli military source, Hezbollah also assists Hamas with bomb production: "They know how to make them more concentrated, what kind of screw to use, how to pack more explosives into less space."[149] Hassan Nasrallah, the secretary-general of Hezbollah, has also declared his support for the ongoing al-Aqsa intifada (Hamas conflict).[150]

Other Alleged Connections. Al-Qaeda, al-Mahdi, and the Palestinian Islamic Jihad Movement have each been alleged to be connected with Hezbollah by various reports. Hezbollah publicly denies these allegations. However, this could be changing, particularly in Iraq. For instance, a *Washington Times* report notes that "Sheik Muqtada al-Sadr, the fiery Iraqi Shi'ite cleric [and al Mahdi leader] who ordered his fanatical militia to attack coalition troops, is being supported by Iran and its terror surrogate Hezbollah."[151] Time will reveal how such terrorist groups intersect in upcoming conflicts in the Middle East and beyond.

What Does All This Mean?

We've learned who the Hezbollah are, what they believe, and their connections, but what does all this mean? Simply put, the Hezbollah are part of the growing Middle East violence deeply rooted in spiritual beliefs—violence that is affecting human lives, oil prices, military decisions, and the economies of other nations, including the United States. In the end, we see that *spiritual beliefs* are at the core of today's conflicts.

12

The Impact of the War in Iraq

"Polls show that a majority believes that the country is, in fact,
now less safe from terrorism because of the war in Iraq."[152]

U.S. NEWS & WORLD REPORT

"WELCOME TO FREE IRAQ. That's what it says on the T-shirts
they sell at Baghdad International Airport. Freedom's great,
but so is security, and right now most Iraqis would trade a
lot of the first for even some of the second."[153]

CNN CORRESPONDENT ANDERSON COOPER

CNN correspondent Anderson Cooper well notes the current situation in Iraq. Iraqi freedom has been won, but security continues to worry most of its citizens. The average American views bombings or raids in Baghdad almost daily on TV newscasts, yet struggles to make sense of the information. What has been the impact of sacred terror on the war in Iraq? For the Christian, how does Iraq's freedom factor into biblical prophecy?

Saddam's Capture

"Ladies and gentlemen, we got him," U.S. administrator Paul Bremer told journalists in Baghdad as loud cheers erupted from Iraqis in the audience. On Saturday, December 13, 2003, Saddam Hussein was found in a tiny cellar at a farmhouse about ten miles south of his hometown Tikrit.

The sequence of events, as described by the U.S. military, was as follows:

- About 600 U.S. forces head to Al-Dawr, south of Tikrit, and conduct intensive searches

- U.S. forces find "rural farmhouse" and cordon off an area of about two km by two km

- "Spider hole" or cellar located in a hut—the narrow hole covered with a rug, bricks and dirt and about six to eight feet (1.8m to 2.5m) deep, with a styrofoam insert

- Saddam Hussein found inside, armed with a pistol, and arrested at 2030 local time (1730 GMT) on Saturday—U.S. says he offers no resistance

- Two unidentified people said to be "close allies" of Saddam Hussein arrested and weapons and more than $750,000 cash confiscated[154]

Saddam Hussein no longer leads the nation he ruled from 1979 to 2003. Saddam and six of his commanders were put on trial for crimes against humanity in the Anfal, (Spoils of War) Campaign between February and August 1988, which prosecutors say left 182,000 Kurds,[155] mostly civilians, dead or missing. Saddam and his cousin Ali Hassan al-Majeed also face a charge of genocide. All face the death penalty, and Saddam has been convicted for crimes against humanity in the killing of some 148 Shiite men from the town of Dujail in the 1980s.[156] Although Saddam has been removed from power, Iraq continues to remain in turmoil.

A Day in Baghdad Today

These are tough times for Mustafa Kubaissy, a 48-year-old shopkeeper in Baghdad. He has been leading a troubled life for the past three years since the US-led invasion of Iraq which ousted former president Saddam Hussein.

"Unfortunately our country has become a mess, with lack of essential items, escalating prices and deteriorating security conditions. The only victims of this disaster are us, innocent people who have started to believe that life under Saddam Hussein's dictatorial regime was much better than it is now," Kubaissy said.

He wakes up at five o'clock in the morning, washes and says his dawn prayers. These days he prefers to pray at home instead of going to his local Sunni mosque in his predominantly Shi'a neighbourhood. As a rule, he has learnt to avoid places of congregation and any crowds. He fears that one day his local mosque could be targeted by Shi'a militants.[157]

Later in the same article, Kubaissy tells the journalist, "Most of my neighbours are Shi'a and they have changed completely towards us. They have become tougher, less educated and some of them have even started telling us that our presence here is dangerous since we are Sunnis and could bring insurgents to our neighbourhood."[158] Americans still tend to view Iraq as a place of military and political turmoil. This is true. What many Americans fail to realize is that Iraq is also a place of tremendous *spiritual turmoil*.

Iraq in Bible Prophecy

One of Saddam Hussein's distinctives was his endeavor to rebuild Babylon. Now that Hussein is no longer in power, that would seem to bring an end to that effort. However, as one observer notes,

> his removal makes the future rebuilding of this city much more feasible. When his regime is removed, the UN, led by the U.S. and Europe, will be doing a great deal of nation building in Iraq and will work hard to create a democratic nation.... Not to mention the fact that Babylon is surrounded by about 60 percent of the world's proven oil reserves (Iraq, Saudi Arabia, Kuwait, and Iran). With Saddam's removal, the Iraqi oil can begin to flow at full capacity, and Iraq will become a very wealthy nation.[159]

A growing number of prophecy scholars believe that the historic city of Babylon will one day become the place of a revived Babylon, will excel economically, and eventually will become the economic and spiritual capital of a future world empire during the Bible's predicted seven-year tribulation. Dr. Mark Hitchcock, in a February 2005 article "Babylon on the Euphrates," describes the possible scenario and how it fits current events:

> Three key events have occurred that are moving Iraq toward democracy.
>
> • Saddam Hussein was removed from power.

- Free elections have been held with a 60 percent turnout.

- An interim government has been established to write a new constitution. The current plan is for elections to occur in December that will elect the permanent members of the new Iraqi parliament.

If Iraq continues on this path, we can expect that European nations (the EU especially) will begin to foster close relations with the new democracy. As these ties grow deeper one could imagine how a great world leader from Europe could use his influence to negotiate some wider presence in Babylon, which just happens to be in the middle of two-thirds of the world's proven oil reserves. (Saudi Arabia, Iraq, Iran, and Kuwait are the world's top four oil producers).[160]

The fact that Babylon is back on the map is intriguing for two key reasons. First, the city of Babylon is the second-most mentioned city in the Bible. It is referred to about 300 times. According to Isaiah 13 and Jeremiah 50–51, Babylon must be destroyed in a way similar to Sodom and Gomorrah. When it is finally destroyed, "the stars of heaven and their constellations will not flash forth their light; the sun will be dark when it rises and the moon will not shed its light" (Isaiah 13:10).

Such destruction has not yet happened in history. Therefore, it must be an event that is still future. It appears from Revelation 14:8 and Revelation 17–18 that the rebuilt city of Babylon will be a great city in the end times and that it will serve as a capital for Antichrist.[161]

Though others believe that the future Babylon could be Rome, New York City, or even the Roman Catholic Church, the most literal interpretation does place Babylon, as described in Revelation, as the central headquarters of the world government at the end of time. Christians who hold to a pretribulational view of the rapture believe that Babylon's rise to dominance will occur after the rapture of the church, and say that an emerging Babylon would be a sign of an imminent return of Christ.

Dr. Charles Dyer published the book *The Rise of Babylon* during the time of the Persian Gulf War in 1991 and exposed Saddam

Hussein's plans to restore the ancient city of Babylon. Dr. Dyer's words, though written some 15 years ago, continue to ring true today when he says,

> Every day that passes brings us closer to the end times, and every day the eyes of the world focus more closely on events in the Middle East and Mesopotamia. One key element in God's program of end-time activities will be the re-establishment of Babylon as a world power. As Babylon takes its place in the center of the world stage, it is time to open our eyes.[162]

The times are still tumultuous, freedom is still tenuous, but the future will be tremendous. Though we don't know when it will happen, the Bible seems to indicate that Babylon will rise again as a major world power. With the support of the United States, the European Union, and the United Nations, along with a democratic government in place in Iraq, such a scenario may not stand too far off in the future.

13

Iran and the Nuclear Countdown

"Iran is obviously part of the problem...."[163]

U.S. PRESIDENT GEORGE W. BUSH,
REGARDING IRAN'S RESPONSE TO A 2006 U.N. RESOLUTION

*"How to handle Iran and, in particular,
its pursuit of nuclear weapons is a problem from Hell."*[164]

KENNETH POLLACK, *THE PERSIAN PUZZLE*

From the President of the United States to the political analyst, the news alerts of our day resound with calls for action with Iran. Why? Iran, with the world's fourth-largest military force, continues to defy U.N. sanctions in its development of nuclear power, which could enable it to launch weapons of mass destruction toward targets hundreds of miles away. Given Iran's official hatred with the nation of Israel, it would not take a rocket scientist, as they say, to figure out where one of Iran's first missiles could be headed. Various sources report:

- Regarding Israel: "Our position toward the Palestinian questions is clear: we say that a nation has been displaced from its own land...."[165]

- "Iran really is making a bid for regional supremacy."[166]

- "For the last three years we have been doing intensive verification in Iran, and even after three years I am not yet in a position to make a judgment on the peaceful nature of Iran's nuclear program" (Mohamed ElBaradei, Director General of the International Atomic Energy Agency, January 2006).[167]

- "Senior officials representing Israel's Ministry of Foreign

Affairs last month privately confided to selected foreign government counterparts that, if the Islamic Republic of Iran completes gas centrifuge facilities at Natanz and begins enriching uranium there, Israel will embark on a military operation to destroy it, according to highly reliable European government sources."[168]

Sound too far-fetched? Consider that Iran's president has publicly declared "the main solution is for the elimination of the Zionist regime Israel"[169] and believes his role is to usher in the end of the world. Consider that Iran plans not only to develop nuclear technology but to share it with other allies (Islamic nations).[170] Consider that Iran has been a key supplier for the Hezbollah movement that has recently been at war with Israel in Southern Lebanon. And consider that U.N. countries holding veto rights continue to stand *against* sanctions on Iran. Such a sensational-sounding scenario may not be too unrealistic after all.

In studying Iran's nuclear potential and spiritual motivations, three areas of concern emerge—Iran's power, Iran's president, and Iran's plans.

Iran's Power

As mentioned earlier, Iran has the fourth-largest military force in the world. In addition to its own military force, Iran supports at least a dozen terror groups in Afghanistan, Iraq, and other places around the globe.[171] Regarding terrorism, there has been much debate as to whether Iran's activities could be considered terrorism. The first problem with determining the answer is that there is no generally accepted definition of terrorism.[172] What we may consider a terrorist act may be considered an act of heroism from another's perspective. However, the evidence seems to stand in favor of Iran as a nation that harbors terrorists and supports acts of terror.

Mortimer Zukerman, editor of *U.S. News & World Report,* wrote in an analysis of Russia's involvement with Iran that "Iran today is the mother of Islamic terrorism."[173] Others studying terrorism at the academic level agree. "Charges of terrorist activities have plagued

Iran from the earliest days of the Islamic revolution to the present. More than any other factor, they have interfered with Iran's ability to establish a responsible foreign policy image."[174]

Not only does Iran have military power through its military and terrorist connections, it also has economic power due to its oil reserves. As one writer notes:

> Iran only pumps about 4 million barrels of crude a day or about 5 percent of the world's daily need. However, Iran is the second largest oil producer among the eleven members of OPEC, and the world's fourth largest exporter of crude oil. Also, Iran says that it plans to up its production from 4 to 7 million barrels a day in the next twenty years, giving it an even larger share of the world's exports and great clout.[175]

In addition to the ability to cut off its own oil supply to the world, Iran also holds the military strength to cut off the transport of oil from surrounding nations with significant oil reserves, including Iraq, Kuwait, and Saudi Arabia. Such a move would be devastating to world oil prices over the long term.

Combine Iran's military might and its potential control over oil supplies with its plans for nuclear development and a hatred for Israel and the United States as its ally, and the nuclear storm that many are beginning to fear begins to sound reasonable. *Very* reasonable.

Iran's President

Born October 28, 1956, Mahmoud Ahmadinejad became the sixth prime minister of Iran on August 3, 2005. Raised in Tehran, Ahmadinejad began his political career by becoming mayor

IRAN'S MILITARY

Eligible age to enter service: 16 for voluntary; 18 for compulsory

Mandatory service terms: 18 months for conscripted service

Manpower in general population fit for military service, males age 18-49: 15,665,725 (2005 estimate)

Manpower reaching eligible age annually, males: 862,056 (2005 estimate)

Military expenditures (in U.S. dollars): $4.3 billion

Percent of GDP: 3.3 percent[176]

of Tehran in 2003 after serving as a professor of civil engineering at Iran's University of Science and Technology. During his run for prime minister, he spoke out against the United Nations and United States and emphasized the development of nuclear technology. These issues, along with his promises to "put the petroleum income onto people's tables," helped bring about his popularity and subsequent election.

Ahmadinejad's most recent publicity spectacle has been his attempts to set up a live debate with President George W. Bush. Initial reports noted, "Iranian President Mahmoud Ahmadinejad has called on U.S. President George W. Bush to participate in a 'direct television debate with us' so Iran can voice its point of view on how to end world predicaments."[177] Shortly thereafter, Ahmadinejad proposed a debate with George W. Bush at the U.N. General Assembly, saying it would be the perfect place for an uncensored discussion the whole world could watch.[178]

But why should we show concern for Ahmadinejad? Ann Leslie's provocative article "Why This Man Should Give Us All Nightmares" describes his theologically driven radicalism:

> But, alas, there's nothing which we would recognise as "reasonable" about President Ahmadinejad, the small, bearded blacksmith's son from the slums of Tehran—who denies the existence of the Holocaust, promises to "wipe Israel off the map" and who, moreover, urges Iranians to "prepare to take over the world."

> The UN gave him until August 31 to reply to its package of proposals designed to stop his nuclear programme. Significantly he chose yesterday to, in effect, reject the UN ultimatum because yesterday was a sacred day in the Islamic calendar.

> It is the day on which the Prophet Mohammed made his miraculous night flight from Jerusalem to heaven and back on Buraq, the winged horse.

> As one Iranian exile told me yesterday: "The trouble with you secular people is that you don't realise how firmly Ahmadinejad believes—literally—in things like the winged horse. By choosing this date for his decision, he is telling his followers that he is going to obey his religious duty.

"And he believes that his religious duty is to create chaos and bloodshed in the 'infidel' world, in order to hasten the return of the Mahdi—the Hidden Imam. So don't expect him to behave, in your eyes, 'reasonably.'"

So who is this Hidden Imam? He was a direct descendant of the Prophet Mohammed who, at the age of five, disappeared down a well around A.D. 940. He will only return after a period of utter chaos and bloodshed, whereupon peace, justice and Islam will reign worldwide.

But according to the political editor of Iran's Resalat newspaper, the President's apocalyptic mindset "makes you very strong. If I think the Mahdi will come in two, three, or four years, why should I be soft? Now is the time to stand strong, to be hard."[179]

In case you are wondering whether this is just the opinion of one journalist, take a look at Ahmadinejad's speech at the United Nations in 2005, where he concluded by calling upon the arrival of the Islamic messiah known as the Hidden Imam or Twelfth Imam, praying, "O mighty Lord, I pray to you to hasten the emergence of your last repository, the Promised One, that perfect and pure human being, the One that will fill this world with justice and peace."[180]

Iran's Plans

Much has been said in the news about Iran's progress toward nuclear obtainment. On August 21, 2006, one day before Iran's self-imposed response to a package regarding a stoppage of uranium enrichment, Iran turned away U.N. inspectors from examining its underground nuclear site, violating the United Nations' Nonproliferation Treaty. Its response? "The Islamic Republic of Iran has made its own decision and in the nuclear case, God willing, with patience and power, will continue its path."[181] Note the Islamic spiritual phrase "God willing." Iran, driven by the radical spiritual beliefs of its prime minister and senior leadership, continues to develop weapons of mass destruction in hopes of bringing about the destruction of Israel and the end of the world.

Such defiance has caused some to conclude the only fitting response would be to sanction or even remove the Ahmadinejad regime before it comes to full nuclear power: "I am increasingly convinced that the only way to protect ourselves from this growing and existential threat is to remove Ahmadinejad and his regime, even if it requires using military force if necessary."[182]

The White House response has been to leave all options on the table. President Bush, on CBS's *Face the Nation,* on January 30, 2006, stated: "Our strategy is to present and hold together a united front to say to the Iranians, 'Your designs to have a nuclear weapon or your desire to have the capability of making a nuclear weapon is unacceptable.'" However, given the current situation in Iraq and a lack of support from key U.N. veto-power members, serious sanctions or military conflict may not occur for some time—something that should be of great concern not only to Americans, but all people.

What About the Bible?

Recently, one prophecy writer noted the role of Iran in the end times:

> Therefore, according to God's Word, the Iranians will join
> with Turkey, the nations of Central Asia, Libya, Sudan, and
> Russia to invade Israel in the end-times. By the way, Iran is
> one of the nations included in President Bush's "axis of evil"
> along with North Korea and Iraq. I hardly have to say much
> to convince anyone today that Iran is an archenemy of Israel
> and the West. Iran is considered by many to be the number
> one rogue nation in the world.[183]

While scholars debate the specifics of this quote, most agree that Iran will continue to be an enemy of Israel into the end times, fitting the contemporary situation. A couple of words of caution should be noted, however.

First, biblical prophecy should not blur our vision in working toward nonviolent solutions with Iran. In other words, even if some believe Iran will be an enemy of Israel in the end times, it does not mean we should not attempt to negotiate peace whenever possible.

The key question for our military and diplomatic leaders at this point is *whether* this is possible and *how* would it be possible.

Second, concern for human life must always stand as a top priority. For example, in the current situation with Iran, we must keep in mind the multitude of innocent civilians who do not support the radical leadership of their country. This is especially true of the minority group of Christians within Iran. How would actions taken against Iran impact the struggling churches of Tehran? How would humanitarian issues be handled? Prophecy is of great concern, and should be, but so should the human lives involved in all aspects and on all sides of the conflict.

C.S. Lewis, in a sermon preached just before the Nazi invasion of Britain, stated well the attitude Christians should have in such circumstances:

> This impending war has taught us some important things. Life is short. The world is fragile. All of us are vulnerable, but we are here because this is our calling. Our lives are rooted not only in time, but also in eternity, and the life of learning, humbly offered to God, is its own reward. It is one of the appointed approaches to the divine reality and the divine beauty, which we shall hereafter enjoy in heaven and which we are called to display even now amidst the brokenness all around us.[184]

14

Is Russia Still a Factor in Today's War on Terror?

"The rapidly intensifying war against Israel—funded, fueled, and driven by proxies of Iran and Syria—poses a critical test for President Bush at the G8 Summit in St. Petersburg. The leader of the free world must make it crystal clear that Vladimir Putin has an urgent choice to make: Russia can choose free markets, free elections, open trade and a peaceful and positive relationship with the West...or it can choose to side with dangerous and diabolical regimes such as Iran and Syria. It cannot do both."[185]

DR. JOEL ROSENBERG, POLITICAL ANALYST AND AUTHOR OF *EPICENTER*

Over the past year, Russia has signed a billion-dollar deal to sell missiles and other weaponry to Iran, despite the fact that much of the West is gravely concerned that Iran is trying to build, buy, or steal nuclear weapons. Further, Russia has agreed to sell missiles to Syria, has resisted U.S. and European efforts to place sanctions on Iran for threatening to annihilate Israel, has agreed to sell arms to the radical Hamas, and passively allowed Iran and Syria to create a formal defensive alliance against the United States, Israel, and moderate Arab regimes in the Middle East.[186]

Russia also hosts the world's only company involved in building nuclear power stations in other nations, with work now being done on plants in Tianwan in China, Kudankulam in India, and Bushehr in Iran. In total, the company Atomstroyexport has 31 reactors within Russia, with plans for several more by 2030.[187]

Most recently, Russia has announced plans to begin work on a power station in northern Turkey,[188] along with new plans to provide a nuclear power station online in the moderate Muslim nation Morocco by 2016, according to AP News reports.[189]

Why should this be of concern? First, Russia's economic partnerships with radical regimes are indirectly supporting the efforts of known terrorist groups. On the evening of September 20, 2001, just days after the devastating events of 9/11, U.S. president George W. Bush proclaimed the new policy of the Bush administration's War on Terror, boldly announcing, "From this day forward, any nation that continues to harbor or support terrorism will be regarded by the United States as a hostile regime."[190] Second, Christians should be on alert due to the amount of attention given to Russia by Bible prophecy scholars who connect today's changing political scene to the events of the end times.

Is Russia Siding with Terror?

Our goal here is not to answer whether Russia is supporting terrorism. Rather, it is to show that Russia's recent political moves have revealed their desire to build economic alliances within countries supporting terrorist activities—activities that are influencing their current attitudes toward War on Terror policies such as the recent discussions to impose sanctions against Iran. For instance, if Russia has over a billion dollars of business at stake within Iran, Syria, and other nations, wouldn't Russian leaders potentially feel caution toward any sanctions that might hurt those partnerships? This seems to clearly be the case.

In addition to development of nuclear power within Iran, Russian weapons have also ended up in some bizarre locations. An AP News report immediately following the Israeli-Hezbollah cease-fire noted that Russian missiles had been launched at the Israeli military by Hezbollah forces. "Israel does not accuse Russia of directly arming Hezbollah, but complains that Russia sold the weapons to Iran and Syria, known supporters of Hezbollah, who then passed them on to the guerrilla group."[191] In testimony before the U.S. Congress as far back as 1993, we discover that missile development by Russia within Iran "has been a conscious policy decision on the part of the Russian government, not some ad-hoc arrangement by unemployed scientists."[192] As one *Reader's Digest* exclusive interview with an Israeli official revealed, "This is not a private operation by some crazy engineers. The contracts [to assist Iran's missile program] have been signed by companies that are at least partially owned by the Russian government."[193]

In a confidential interview in Germany, a former Iranian intelligence officer confirmed Western intelligence reports that Russians began working on Iran's long-range missile projects in 1994. At that time, Russian technicians visited the top-secret Iranian Defense Technology and Science Research Center near Karaj, 50 miles northwest of Tehran. Iran subsequently began receiving assistance from Russia's state-run missile plants and technical universities. Russian advisers worked at Iran's missile plants in Esfahan and Semnan, as well as at design centers in Sultanatabad, Lavizan, and Kuh-e Bagh-e-Melli on the outskirts of the capital. "After that, Iran's missile program jelled," says Patrick Clawson, an Iran analyst at the National Defense University in Washington, D.C.[194]

The big picture does not indicate a healthy scenario. It is evident Russia is building nuclear power stations within Iran and other nations that have strong potential evil intent regarding their usage, holds deep economic partnerships with nations that desire to annihilate Israel, and has supplied weapons that have been used in recent military conflicts (likely through third party distributors),[195] and yet Russia continues to stand against sanctions designed to discourage Iranian nuclear development. The United Nations, European Union, and United States will continue to disagree with Russia on Mideast peace issues as a result, which may lead to greater problems in the future.

What Does the Bible Say About Russia?

The aforementioned scenarios have led many to speculate about Russia's role in biblical prophecy. Beyond even religious scholarship, the Russian newspaper *Pravda* has cast its own scenario for a nuclear apocalypse in the Middle East:

1. The war in Lebanon continues to flare.

2. Hezbollah fires Iranian missiles at Israel, but Israel intercepts those missiles, as it intercepted the Scuds fired in 1991 by Iraq.

3. Israel attacks Iranian nuclear sites, perhaps with the help of the U.S. Navy. Iran launches a full-scale counterattack against Israeli cities and American warships.

4. Turkey gets dragged into the war, as does Russia, and all Hell breaks loose.

"Such a scenario does not seem too unrealistic to me," Sergey Markov, a Russian political scientist, told *Pravda.* "These days anything is possible in the Middle East. People living there are crazy and they constantly keep playing with fire. Their situation has gone out of control and is ready to explode any minute. In fact, the new world war is already going in that place."[196]

Pravda may not realize how accurate its article could be. According to Ezekiel 38–39, a group of nations will rise up to destroy Israel in a yet-unfulfilled prophecy, with God intervening in the end to pour out judgment and redeem Israel. While there is much debate over the identity of the nations described in Ezekiel 38–39, many agree that Russia will, in some major way, serve as one of the key nations, along with Turkey, Iran, and others.[197] In *The Prophecy That Is Shaping History,* Jon Mark Ruthven acknowledges, "Easily one of the most neglected but powerfully galvanizing forces shaping history in the world today is the prophecy of Gog and Magog [Russia] from the 38th and 39th chapters of the book of Ezekiel."[198]

Another major point of contention is whether these events are to occur before or after the rapture of the church. Either way, the groundwork for these events would likely be put into place years earlier, laying a foundation that even Russia's *Pravda* newspaper can figure out.

In an interview about Ezekiel 38–39, Dr. Joel Rosenberg, who served as an advisor to former Israeli prime minister Benjamin Netanyahu, shared:

The turning point for me came in 2000, when I was hired

as a senior communications adviser to former Israeli prime minister Benjamin Netanyahu and former deputy prime minister Natan Sharansky. I was on a flight from Washington to New York with Sharansky when he began telling me a story I will never forget. He explained how a few years earlier Netanyahu had sent him on a mission to Moscow to hold private talks with Russian Foreign Minister Primakov and the head of the KGB (now called the FSB), Vladimir Putin. The reason: to express Israel's concern that Russian nuclear scientists and Russian nuclear warheads might fall into the hands of radical Middle Eastern regimes such as Iraq or Iran.

...Was it really possible that the prime minister of Israel and his top advisers were worried about a Russian-Iranian military alliance, and a nuclear one at that? Were events being set into motion for the fulfillment of Ezekiel 38 and 39?[199]

Here we find current events and biblical prophecy colliding in a way that seems more than coincidental. Based on the evidence, it appears the road is being paved for a future fulfillment that in some way includes the modern-day nation of Russia. As prophecy expert Dr. John Walvoord observed, "Never before has it seemed more likely that the prediction will be fulfilled given by Ezekiel (chapters 38 and 39) of an invasion from the north."[200]

Islam's Perspective

Interestingly, Islam has its own version of Ezekiel 38–39, not identified as Gog and Magog, but as the war of Yjuj and Majuj, which is strangely different from the Old Testament's rendering. They are mentioned both in Surahs 18:96 and 21:96 in the Qur'an, teaching that its version of Gog and Magog is number four of ten signs that will take place during the end times.

According to Islamic teaching, Gog and Magog are "two groups of Turks that were spreading corruption through the earth during the time of Abraham. Finally, to keep them in check, they were enclosed behind a great barrier."[201] Unable to move, they turn to attack Muslims in Jerusalem. Jesus prays against Gog and Magog, and Allah destroys them through deadly disease.

In a strange twist, the Islamic prophecy is in agreement with the biblical prophecy of Jews and Christians that the Islamic nations will attack Israel in the last days.

How Should We Respond?

If, as the research indicates, Russia is assisting rogue nations with military technology and economic partnerships, our government should be encouraged to confront Russian officials, noting the potential for economic sanctions if no changes are made. As former U.S. undersecretary of defense Paul Wolfowitz says of Russia, "It must be made clear that doing business with our enemies will cost them if they want to do business with us."[202] Further, U.S. laws require the President to impose sanctions on countries that assist certain nations in building ballistic missiles and nuclear weapons. Simply acknowledging the need to enforce already-existing laws could be a solid place to start.

For individual Christians there are two ways to respond. First, knowledge should drive us to more intelligent and diligent prayer. The thought that America's former Cold War enemy continues to arm enemies of the United States and Israel should motivate us to more fervent prayer for the safety of the nations involved, wisdom for our government's leaders, and support for our troops. Second, as should already be the case, we must make the most of every opportunity. The apostle Paul said it well when he wrote, "Be very careful, then, how you live—not as unwise but as wise, making the most of every opportunity, because the days are evil."[203]

15

The European Union and the Future of World Government

"The [European] Union must become the most competitive and dynamic knowledge-based economy in the world capable of sustainable economic growth with more and better jobs and greater social cohesion."[204]

EUROPEAN COUNCIL, LISBON, MARCH 2000

"If considered a single unit, the European Union has the largest economy in the world."[205]

INTERNATIONAL MONETARY FUND

"It is entirely possible that people will discover that democracy does not have the answer to our world's problems and may succumb to dictatorship, exactly as the Bible predicts for the end of the age."[206]

JOHN WALVOORD

In 2002, I (John) produced my first television program focusing on the role of the European Union in the Middle East. At the time, the United States, Russia, European Union, and United Nations were gathering to discuss the War on Terror and the Roadmap for Peace in the Middle East. Journalist Dr. Jimmy DeYoung and I discussed these issues in-depth both on camera and off the record in a way that has marked my thinking ever since. Of greatest importance to me was the answer to the question, "Why in the world is the European Union involved in talks about the Middle East?" My growing conclusion since that time is that a spiritual dynamic is at root, with Bible prophecy unfolding before our very eyes.

Islam in Europe

In our conversations on this matter, Dr. DeYoung mentioned the growing emergence of Islam in European nations. "There is an underlying factor that must be understood as it relates to the European Union. Politically, they are very conscious of the Islamic influence they have within their own countries. There is a large population of Islamic people from all over the world, particularly the Middle East, who have come to live in their countries, which means the potential for terrorism is very prevalent in these European nations as well.

"When you look at the European Union, it basically comes down on the side of the Palestinians of the Arab world. The European Union is going to be a key player in the end times. The Bible talks about a revived Roman Empire—Daniel chapter 7 talks about a revived Roman Empire having ten horns. The ten horns will become ten units of some type that will come together and form this revived Roman Empire from which the Antichrist will come."

A United Currency

At the time of this writing, one U.S. dollar currently equals about €1.26 (euros). This may not seem like much difference, but it adds up quickly. A semester of college education in Europe that might cost a local student €15,000 would cost over $19,000. A car that costs €25,000 would cost $31,720. Airline tickets, hotel rooms, restaurants, and other travel expenses continue to cost Americans more in much of Europe.

I (Dillon) had a relative serving for a year as a missionary in Western Europe and discovered that financially supporting a European missionary has become increasingly difficult. According to a 2001 report by Youth with a Mission, an increasing number of American missionaries in Europe are obtaining local jobs upon arrival to help offset the rising cost of missionary expenses.[207] The emerging role of "marketplace missionaries" has been partly influenced by the power of Europe's strong united currency.

As Jimmy DeYoung put it, "There has never been a common currency in that geographical location of the world since the Roman

Empire, when the denarius was the common currency. One of the indicators that we have an infrastructure for the revived Roman Empire is the fact that they have a common currency and a parliamentary system that's operating—the European Parliament. We're seeing the infrastructure of the revived Roman Empire come together in what we know today as the European Union and thus we're going to continue to see its influence grow because prophecy says they will be a major player in the end times."

Making Peace

Several peace treaties already exist in the Middle East, yet violence continues to rage. Whether the Camp David Accords, the Oslo Accord, the Palestinian/Israeli agreement, or even the Israeli-Hezbollah cease-fire, lasting peace fails to be achieved. According to DeYoung, "The Bible says that in the last days the Antichrist, that world ruler, will come on the scene. In Daniel 9:27 we read that 'he will confirm a covenant with many for one seven'—or seven years. I used to say that when the Antichrist signs a peace agreement with Israel, we know we're in that time. That's not what the Word of God says.

"That word 'confirm' is *gabar* in Hebrew. It doesn't mean sign. It means 'strengthen, make stronger, confirm.' The peace agreements are on the table. They are waiting for a superpower to come on the scene who says, 'I can confirm that.' At least one portion of the peace agreement of Daniel 9:27 already exists and is waiting for the Antichrist to confirm it. All that we see taking place today is playing into this end-times scenario laid out in God's Word."

The Oil Issue

While we discussed oil in an earlier chapter, it is important here to note *European* dependence on oil. According to a 2000 European Wind Energy Association report, 45 percent of EU oil imports originated from the Middle East, with projections of over 90 percent of oil being imported by 2030.[208] According to DeYoung, "All these other [oil-producing] countries are key players in the end times, key players today politically, and they can use that as leverage on these national leaders and on these different nations to do what they want them to do as it relates to Israel. That's part of this whole picture as well."

Years before the war in Iraq, prophecy expert Dr. John Walvoord observed, "Europe's industrialized nations must have a secure, guaranteed flow of oil. Europe's need may result in a special economic and political agreement."[209] His words appear to be increasingly true today.

The European Union and Israel

Some have also noted the growing concerns between the EU and Israel as an emerging trend moving toward a revived Roman Empire that opposes Israel. While this is certainly not the present case, a brief look at the topics of today's news shows reveals the following:

- "EU accuses Israel of 'disproportionate use of force' in Lebanon," *USA Today*, July 13, 2006.[210]

- "Israel is set on a collision course with the European Union and could turn into a pariah state like South Africa during the apartheid years, if the Mideast conflict is not resolved."[211]

- *"Israel and U.S. Labeled Biggest Threats to World Peace."* Over half of Europeans think that Israel now presents the biggest threat to world peace, according to a controversial poll requested by the European Commission.[212]

I (Dillon) have been surprised by the clearly evident personal biases in the views. For instance, a Scottish writer sees Europe as dominant (Robert Congdon and other European prophecy writers);[213] a Jewish writer finds the ten nations all in the Middle East (in Psalm 83!);[214] and Americans often find a "world" government (such as Thomas Ice)[215] that includes the United States. Regardless, almost all the models include the European Union as a major player of the end times in some way.

It is impossible to know for certain if the European Union is the embryonic form of the government that will ally itself with a final global religion as described in Revelation 17. However, at the very least, it serves as a powerful example of just how such an alliance could develop.[216]

Part 4

What Does Bible Prophecy Say About the Middle East Meltdown?

"Surely the Sovereign LORD does nothing without revealing his plan to his servants the prophets."

AMOS 3:7

This next section will give you the opportunity to discover what God's Word reveals about the end times and the Middle East conflicts of our day. We'll leap across the mountain peaks of history and then plunge into God's future for Israel and His church. Along the way, we'll find that today's events position us nearer to God's glorious kingdom than any other time in history.

Mark Twain once wrote, "The art of prophecy is very difficult, especially with respect to the future."[217] While humorous in approach, his words are true. Prophecy is not an easy area to understand, but it *is* understandable. The God who shared His future through His prophets and apostles is preparing to shower future blessings upon His church and Israel after generations of suffering and perseverance. Ultimately, they will be blessed beyond all human understanding.

16

Why Study Bible Prophecy?

*"The greatest purpose of the prophetic Word, as designed by
God, is the pursuit of holiness by His people. This is every-
where evident in one prophetic passage after another. Check
all the passages dealing with the return of the Lord and you
will find that, almost without exception, our Lord's return is
used as a basis for an exhortation to godliness."*[218]

J. Hampton Keathley, III

I (John) was once asked to speak and answer the question, Why
study Bible prophecy? As I evaluated why the study of prophecy
is critical for all people and especially those who follow Christ, I
developed seven significant reasons for such study. As we enter the
section of this book that focuses on the Bible's words regarding the
current Middle East conflict and terrorism, it's appropriate for us to
consider these seven reasons:

1. Prophecy Is God Speaking Directly to Humanity

Exactly how much of the Bible is comprised of prophecy? In sur-
veying the Old and New Testaments, we find that...

- Approximately 27 percent of the entire Bible contains prophetic material. Half of that has already been fulfilled, and
  half remains to be fulfilled.

- Of the Old Testament's 23,210 verses, 6,641 contain prophetic
  material, or 28.5 percent.

- Of the New Testament's 7,914 verses, 1,711 contain prophetic
  material, or 21.5 percent.

- Of the Bible's 31,124 verses, 8,352 contain prophetic material, or 27 percent of the whole Bible.
- There are 1,800 verses that deal with the second coming of Christ.
- In the New Testament, 318 verses deal with the second coming of Christ.
- Every twenty-fifth verse in the New Testament refers to the second coming.[219]

The Bible declares itself to be direct revelation from God. The apostle Peter wrote, "Above all, you must understand that no prophecy of Scripture came about by the prophet's own interpretation. For prophecy never had its origin in the will of man, but men spoke from God as they were carried along by the Holy Spirit."[220] Why is this significant? One verse earlier, Peter says, "You will do well to pay attention to it [prophecy], as to a light shining in a dark place, until the day dawns and the morning star rises in your hearts."

Prophecy makes up a major portion of the Bible. Would we want to face God someday and admit that we did not believe prophecy was important? Certainly God desires such a significant portion of Scripture to be studied and understood by its readers.

2. God Himself Commands Us to Study Prophecy

In Isaiah 45:21, the prophet wrote,

> Who foretold this long ago, who declared it from the distant past? Was it not I, the LORD? And there is no God apart from me, a righteous God and a Savior, there is none but me. Turn to me and be saved, all you ends of the earth; for I am God and there is no other.

God has not only provided prophecy. He has *commanded* us to study it.

The apostle Paul wrote, "All Scripture is inspired by God and is useful to teach us what is true and to make us realize what is wrong with our lives. It straightens us out and teaches us to do what is right. It is God's way of preparing us in every way, fully equipped for every good thing God wants us to do."[221] If *all* Scripture is inspired by God and useful, then this must refer to all prophecy as well.

3. Jesus Personally Encouraged the Study of Prophecy

Jesus clearly communicated that it's important to study prophecy. Mark 13 reveals this emphasis Jesus gave to His followers to understand the predictions of the Bible:

Mark 13:5—"Jesus said to them: 'Watch out that no one deceives you.'"

Mark 13:9—"You must be on your guard."

Mark 13:23—"So be on your guard; I have told you everything ahead of time."

Mark 13:29—"When you see these things happening, you know that it is near, right at the door."

Mark 13:33—"Be on guard! Be alert! You do not know when that time will come."

Mark 13:37—"What I say to you, I say to everyone: 'Watch!'"

Not only did Christ give these positive warnings, He also called "foolish" those who did not study and believe what God said, especially regarding His future teachings. After His resurrection, He instructed two men during a walk to Emmaus, saying, "'How foolish you are, and how slow of heart to believe all that the prophets have spoken! Did not the Christ have to suffer these things and then enter his glory?' And beginning with Moses and all the Prophets,

VIEWS TOWARD THE BIBLE

Rationalism: Human reasoning as more important than the Bible's revelation.

Mysticism: Bible interpretation based on personal experiences or feelings.

Romanism: The Roman Catholic Church declares the right interpretation of Scripture.

Neo-Orthodoxy: The Bible is authoritative only when it speaks to a person personally.

Cultism: The Bible, *along with other spiritual books,* is authoritative.

Protestantism: The Bible alone is God's divine word to humanity.[222]

he explained to them what was said in all the Scriptures concerning himself."[223]

As prophecy expert Lehman Strauss has noted,

> A very striking and strange condition exists at present, namely, the deliberate refusal on the part of religious and political leaders to consult carefully the prophetic Scriptures. True, there have been cranks, blind fanatics, hobby-riders and unwise date-setters posing as prophetic teachers, but all of these unscholarly obscurantists put together do not afford any man a legitimate excuse for not studying the divine plan as it is plainly set forth in the Bible.[224]

4. Prophecy Is Evidence That God Exists

As mentioned earlier, 27 percent of the Bible is prophetic in nature. That's 8,352 verses! All it takes is one false prophecy to discredit the claim that the Bible is God's Word to us. Yet the fact no prophecy of Scripture (of the prophecies fulfilled so far) has been proven false serves as confirmation of God's trustworthiness and existence. "In all the writings of the world, the accuracy of biblical prophecy is unique and stands as one of the great evidences of the God-breathed nature of the Bible."[225]

The prophet Isaiah stated this from God's point of view when he wrote:

> This is what the LORD says—
>   Israel's King and Redeemer, the LORD Almighty:
> I am the first and I am the last;
>   apart from me there is no God.
>
> Who then is like me? Let him proclaim it.
>   Let him declare and lay out before me
> what has happened since I established my ancient people,
>   and what is yet to come—
>   yes, let him foretell what will come.
>
> Do not tremble, do not be afraid.
>   Did I not proclaim this and foretell it long ago?
> You are my witnesses. Is there any God besides me?
>   No, there is no other Rock; I know not one.[226]

Knowing that the reliability of prophecy helps confirm God's very existence and the unique nature of Scripture should compel us to study it for our personal spiritual growth and for sharing with others.

5. Prophecy Gives Us Hope for the Future

Dr. Wilbur M. Smith suggested that there are three different attitudes one can take toward the future. The first is *indifference,* the second is *fear,* and the third is *hope.* No intelligent person would take the first, no one needs to be trapped in the second, and all can possess the third. There is comfort and hope for all believers who love and study the prophecies of the Bible.[227]

The flip side of hope is fear. While today's acts of terror have brought greater fear to everyday life, God's Word, including prophecy, provides a hope for a better future. As 9/11 widow Lisa Beamer noted:

> Personally, I'm less afraid now than I was before September 11, because I have a greater sense of God's sovereignty. He's in control, and he has a plan for the world. Not only that, he has plans for me individually. And he loves me more than any human being ever could love me. So what's really to fear?[228]

First Corinthians 14:3 teaches, "Everyone who prophesies speaks to men for their strengthening, encouragement and comfort." Prophecy's intent is to help individuals and communities of people to be encouraged regarding God's future for the world. As the apostle Peter said, "In keeping with his promise we are looking forward to a new heaven and a new earth, the home of righteousness. So then, dear friends, since you are looking forward to this, make every effort to be found spotless, blameless and at peace with him."[229] For followers of Christ, the future is not a source of horror, but a source of hope.

6. Prophecy Encourages a Lifestyle of Integrity

"Believers in the early church held vigorously to belief in the

imminent coming of Jesus Christ, and that belief powerfully motivated them to holy living."[230] The apostle John was an example of this
when he wrote, "Dear friends, now we are children of God, and what
we will be has not yet been made known. But we know that when he
appears, we shall be like him, for we shall see him as he is. Everyone
who has this hope in him purifies himself, just as he is pure."[231] As Dr.
Tim LaHaye observes regarding the study of the book of Revelation,
"I have found that the proper understanding of Revelation motivates Christians to consistent dedication and service."[232] Prophecy
is a *motivator* of holy living.

The phrase "we shall be like him, for we shall see him as he is"
indicates the key hope of the Christian afterlife. It marks top songs
such as "I Can Only Imagine"; drives the plot of bestselling fiction
such as *The Rapture;* and emerges from every Christian funeral
service as *the reason* for our enduring faith. Regarding the aforementioned verses from 1 John 3:2-3, *The NET Bible* explains how
this could occur:

> The phrase *we will be like him, because we will see him just
> as he is* has been explained two ways: (1) believers will really
> become more like God than they now are, and will do this
> through seeing God as he really is; or (2) believers will realize
> that they are already like God, but did not realize it until they
> see him as he is. One who sees a strong emphasis on realized
> eschatology in the Gospel of John and the Epistles might
> opt for the second view, since it downplays the difference
> between what believers already are in the present age and
> what they will become in the next. It seems better, though, in
> light of the statement in 3:2a that "what we will be has not yet
> been revealed" and because of the reference to Christ's *par-
> ousia* in 2:28, that the author intends to distinguish between
> the present state of believers and what they will be like in
> the future. Thus the first view is better, that believers really
> will become more like God than they are now, as a result of
> seeing him as he really is.[233]

Someone said, "A good character is the best tombstone. Those
who loved you, and were helped by you, will remember you. So carve

your name on hearts, and not on marble." That someone was C.H. Spurgeon, the brilliant nineteenth-century British pastor whose life marked countless others as he proclaimed the future hope of prophecy's fulfillment.[234] To fully embrace the belief that Jesus could return at any moment fuels a lifestyle of integrity.

7. Prophecy Shapes Our Personal Thinking and Worldview

"It [the rapture] should make a major difference in every Christian's values, actions, priorities, and goals."[235] No one can be unconcerned about the end of the world, especially if God is the One who has purposely revealed this information in the Bible. It is important that we know and understand God's message to us.

A.W. Tozer once remarked, "The man who comes to a right belief about God is relieved of ten thousand temporal problems for he sees at once that these have to do with matters which at the most cannot concern him very long."[236] When we see prophecy as the fulfillment of God's plan for the universe, our concern is not whether these are "The Last Days on Earth," as argued by scholars on the ABC special report on 20/20, but rather, it's helping others see how the pieces of today's events fit into the larger context of the Bible.[237]

Three specific applications can then follow. Dr. Tim LaHaye makes an important point in his book *Are We Living in the End Times?* In the past, when people have taken prophecy seriously, it has led to three things: 1) It has challenged believers to holy living in an unholy age; 2) it has given Christians a greater motivation to evangelize; and 3) it has caused the church to be more missionary-minded from the realization it must fulfill the great commission before Christ returns.[238]

Now that we see the great importance of studying Bible prophecy, let's see what we can learn about how Bible prophecy relates to today's Middle East meltdown.

17

Religion in the Last Days

"We're now at the dawn of an era in which an extreme fanatical religious ideology, undeterred by the usual calculations of prudence and self-preservation, is wielding state power and will soon be wielding nuclear power."[239]

CHARLES KRAUTHAMMER

What does the Bible say about the last days? Given that the Bible is nearly one-fourth prophecy, the answer is that it says a lot! But if we were to try to somehow summarize the Bible's teachings on the last days, it's possible to condense them into ten key points—and every one of these ten is becoming increasingly evident in today's headlines.

Several of the points emerge from Paul's words to his young protégé Timothy, then the leader of the growing church at Ephesus. In 1 Timothy 4:1, Paul reveals that…

1. People Will Depart from the Faith

"The Spirit clearly says that in later times some will abandon the faith." What is *the* faith? In the Greek text, the word "the" in front of "faith" is a definite article—"the" faith refers to the essential doctrines, the foundational truths that make up Christianity.

What are some examples of these foundational truths? Here are several:

- The divine nature of Christ
- The atoning death of Christ on the cross for our sins
- The physical resurrection of Christ from the dead

- The promise of the resurrection of all believers
- The doctrine of the Trinity
- Christ's imminent second coming

The Bible warns that in the last days there will be a major departure from these foundational biblical truths.

Is this happening today? *Pulpit Helps* reported the significant findings of a survey of 7,441 Protestant pastors who responded to the question: "Do you believe in the physical resurrection of Jesus from the dead?" The results showed that 51 percent of Methodists, 35 percent of Presbyterians, 30 percent of Episcopalians, and 33 percent of American Baptists *did not believe in the physical resurrection of Jesus from the dead.*[240]

It is devastating to think that pastors can continue serving in the ministry even though they deny such a foundational doctrine to the Christian faith. This very point was brought home to me (John) during a debate I held between Bishop John Shelby Spong, an Episcopalian bishop from Newark who was the first bishop to ordain homosexuals into the church, and the late Protestant scholar, Dr. Walter Martin, author of the bestselling *Kingdom of the Cults.* This debate was held in 1989 in Dallas, Texas.

During the debate, Bishop Spong answered negative comments about his beliefs by responding, "What I said in my book was that the simplistic claim that Jesus is God is not affirmed in Scripture.... What the Christian narrative, it seems to me, says, is that God was in Christ; that when we meet Christ, we meet God."

Dr. Walter Martin did not buy Spong's theory. He turned and looked at the audience, "I think what we are dealing with is what is called theobabble. The bishop makes a clear statement that Jesus is not God. Then, when asked about it, he replies 'That's not what I meant.' The problem is that the Episcopal doctrine of the Trinity says that Jesus is God the Son, the second person of the Trinity. When the bishop took his ordination vows, the bishop said, 'I will obey Jesus Christ.' The bishop said he would be subject to the authority of the Scriptures. The Scriptures clearly say Jesus is God the Son. Every time he celebrates the Eucharist in the Episcopal Church, he is affirming John chapter 1. Even though he may not want to believe it, he's doing it…. To make such statements that He is not God, however you equivocate afterwards, is to do great disservice to the Lord you swore, when you were ordained, that you would defend."

Another area in which people are abandoning the faith is the central belief that Jesus is the risen Son of God. According to the most recent Barna survey, 39 percent of the American population can be defined as "Notional Christians." Barna defines Notional Christians

> as those who describe themselves as Christians, but do not believe that they will have eternal life because of their reliance upon the death and resurrection of Jesus Christ and the grace extended to people through a relationship with Christ. (A large majority of these individuals believe they will have eternal life, but not because of a grace-based relationship with Jesus Christ.)[241]

A Newsweek/Beliefnet poll revealed that a shocking number of people who call themselves *evangelical* and *born-again* have come to reject those words. The question in the poll read: "Can a good person who isn't of your religious faith go to heaven or attain salvation, or not?" According to the poll, comprised of more than 1,000 adults 18 years of age and older, 68 percent of evangelical Christians believe "good" people of other faiths can also go to heaven. Nationally, 79 percent of those surveyed said the same thing, with an astounding 91-percent agreement among Catholics. Beliefnet spokesman Steven Waldman called the results "pretty amazing."[242]

The results of these polls reveal that people are, in fact, departing from the faith. Such Christianity resembles the lukewarm church at Laodicea that John mentions in Revelation 3:14-22.

2. Evil Spirits Will Mislead People

Going back to 1 Timothy 4:1, Paul adds that in later times, people will also "follow deceiving spirits." He is talking not about politics, money, or oil, but *spiritual* battles. In 2006 Barna observed that more than half of adults say that the devil, or Satan, is not a living being but a symbol of evil. And 45 percent of professedly *born-again Christians* deny Satan's existence. Slightly more than two-thirds of Catholics (68 percent) say the devil is nonexistent and only a symbol of evil.[243] When the majority of those in our culture and nearly a majority of American Christians do not even believe Satan or demonic spirits are real, it would seem that Paul's warning about demons deceiving people is being fulfilled.

When I (John) read 1 Timothy 4:1 in graduate school, I thought I would never have to deal with deceiving spirits in my ministry. Was I ever wrong! In the very first television debate I ever conducted, leaders from a group called Eckankar calmly told me they had conversations with spirits every day. And over the 26 years I've been telecasting debates, documentaries, and interviews, it seems that about every third program has guests who say they are getting information from spirits.

For example, several years ago I received a letter from José Silva of Silva Mind Control. He has a course on how he invites two of his spirit guides to help people solve their problems. He said he would be interested in coming on our program. I wanted to find out more so I could help others deal with what I believed was a trap. I set up a debate with José Silva and two Christian scholars. We had a packed audience and while the television cameras were rolling, I asked José, "In order for you to get this information, you must have experienced it yourself. Do you have psychic guides?"

Silva replied, "I've had them all my life."

I asked him, "Do they talk to you?"

He calmly responded, "I got the idea to pass them on to others, because I was helped from this source."

"So you had the psychic guides as counselors helping you formulate this course since day one?"

Silva: "That is correct."

Next I asked, "Do they give you information about the future?"

I'll never forget what he said. "Anytime you find yourself with a problem and you do not know what to do next, you can consult them. They are here to help you become as good as they are."[244] Silva admitted that he received his mind control course from spirits who spoke to him, and this course has been passed on to millions of people.

What's frightening about this is that multitudes of people are being led astray by what the Bible would define as evil spirits.

3. People Will Follow the Teachings of Demons

The apostle Paul goes on in 1 Timothy 4:1 to predict the end times will be marked by "things taught by demons." What are these teachings? Paul speaks on only two other occasions about demons. The first contrasts demons with angels (Romans 8:38). The second, in 1 Corinthians 10:20-21, equates offering sacrifices to other gods with sacrifices to demons. In other words, the teachings of demons would certainly include teachings about gods other than Jesus Christ.

Using this definition, we can easily see how Paul's predictions are coming to pass before our very eyes. There are more different religious movements today than in any other time in recent history.

Today's religious climate definitely finds itself promoting acceptance of any and all religious groups in the pursuit of political correctness. In doing so, our culture is helping to fulfill the apostle Paul's prophecies of 2,000 years ago.

4. People Will Not Put Up with Those Who Teach Sound Doctrine

Paul, in his second letter to Timothy, warned that "the time will come when men will not put up with sound doctrine."[245] Sound doctrine is made up of the essential teachings of Jesus and the apostles, and includes essentials such as Christ's virgin birth, His sinless life, His deity, His death, burial, resurrection, and ascension, and His promised future return.

Interestingly, these essentials are ridiculed by scholars in books such as *Misquoting Jesus, The Jesus Dynasty, What Jesus Meant,* and *The Jesus Papers;* fiction such as *The Da Vinci Code;*[246] and television documentaries on ABC, National Geographic, and The History Channel. Barbara Thiering's book *Jesus the Man* pushes to even further extremes, arguing in a *nonfiction* work that her research on the Dead Sea Scrolls and the Gospels proves that Jesus was the leader of a radical faction of Essene priests, was not of virgin birth, did not die on the cross, married Mary Magdalene, fathered a family, later divorced, and died sometime after A.D. 64.[247] Clearly, we live in a time when an increasing number of people will not put up with the orthodox teachings of Christianity.

5. People Will Hear What They *Want* to Hear, Not the Truth They *Need* to Hear

"Instead, to suit their own desires, they will gather around them a great number of teachers to say what their itching ears want to hear."[248] While many churches continue to faithfully communicate the true message of Jesus, thousands of others have individually or corporately rejected the central beliefs of the Christian faith. When a denomination rejects the authority of God's Word, accepts sinful lifestyle behaviors as normative for members and clergy, and sexual sin and divorce runs rampant even among "mature" believers, it is only reasonable to believe that Paul's predictions are coming true.

As early as 1994, *Newsweek* reported that among those attending evangelical churches "people have developed a pick and choose Christianity in which individuals take what they want…and pass over what does not fit their spiritual goals. What many have left behind is a pervasive sense of sin."[249]

The growing biblical illiteracy of Americans also confirms the direction our culture is headed. Only 40 percent of Americans can name more than four of the Ten Commandments, and a scant half can cite any of the four authors of the Gospels. Twelve percent believe Joan of Arc was Noah's wife. And three out of four Americans believe the Bible teaches that "God helps those who help themselves."[250]

While the rapture of the church could happen today or a thousand years from today, the signs Paul predicted in the first-century church seem to indicate we are drawing very close to the last days.

6. People Will Base Their Religious Beliefs on Fiction

The apostle Paul alerts us about the source of authority for those who are misled in the last days: "They will turn their ears away from the truth and turn aside to myths."[251] The "myths" mentioned here are fictional stories. Fiction can have very positive, instructive elements, as Jesus illustrated through His parables. Yet fiction can also serve as a powerful vehicle for *un*truth.

Paul's prediction communicates that in contrast with believing what is true, many people will believe stories lacking a factual basis. Take for example Martin Scorsese, director of the 2006 hit film *The Departed* and several other films. But among those films includes an extremely controversial motion picture on the life of Christ built upon the fictional story found in Nikos Kazantzaki's novel, *The Last Temptation of Christ*. I (John) watched this movie in a Hollywood premiere in which Scorsese had Jesus say, "I was never crucified, I never came back from the dead. I'm a man like everyone else. Why are you telling these lies?"

Scorsese then had Paul respond, "I created the truth out of what people needed and what they believed. If I have to crucify you to save the world, then I'll crucify you. If I have to resurrect you, then I'll do that too, whether you like it or not."

Scorsese and Kazantzaki followed the lead of liberal theologians in inventing a story about Jesus, assuming that Paul didn't really meet the resurrected Christ. But this makes Jesus a fraud and Paul a liar who simply made up a Jesus of his own liking to meet the needs of people. It flatly denies 1 Corinthians 15:3-8, where Paul wrote,

> I delivered to you as of first importance what I also received, that Christ died for our sins according to the Scriptures, and that He was buried, and that He was raised on the third day according to the Scriptures, and that He appeared to Cephas, then to the twelve. After that He appeared to more than five hundred brethren at one time…. then He appeared to James, then to all the apostles; and last of all…He appeared to me also (NASB).

In a culture where many top-selling books and films are of a spiritual yet distinctly non-Christian nature, the truth of Christ's resurrection has come under great attack. Unfortunately, movies such as *Signs, Sixth Sense,* and *The Da Vinci Code* have provided the extent of theological training for many Americans, unchurched *and* churched.

7. There Will Be Church Leaders Who Deny Jesus Christ

The apostle Peter also wrote about the signs of the last days. In 2 Peter 2:1-2 we find this: "There were also false prophets among the people, just as there will be false teachers among you. They will secretly introduce destructive heresies, even denying the sovereign Lord who bought them—bringing swift destruction on themselves. Many will follow their shameful ways and will bring the way of truth into disrepute."

The *New York Times* featured a front-page article about the pastor of a 1,000-member Reformed church in Michigan by the name of Richard A. Rhem. After 25 years of ministry he told his congregation that he no longer believed that faith in Jesus was the only way to salvation. Therefore, his denomination tried to fire him.

How did the members in his congregation react? The congregation voted to withdraw from their denomination and stay with their pastor. In doing so, they followed their pastor in departing from the Christian faith.[252]

While we do not want to diminish the amazing impact of countless spiritual leaders today, the Bible does declare that many church leaders will come to deny the fundamental truth of Christianity—that Jesus is the Christ. In 2004, Barna's research revealed this very definite trend:

> Based on interviews with 601 Senior Pastors nationwide, representing a random cross-section of Protestant churches, Barna reports that only half of the country's Protestant pastors—51%—have a biblical worldview. Defining such a worldview as believing that absolute moral truth exists, that it is based upon the Bible, and having a biblical view on six core beliefs (the accuracy of biblical teaching, the sinless nature of Jesus, the literal existence of Satan, the omnipotence and omniscience of God, salvation by grace alone, and the personal responsibility to evangelize), the researcher produced data showing that there are significant variations by denominational affiliation and other demographics.

"The most important point," Barna argued, "is that you can't give people what you don't have. The low percentage of Christians who have a biblical worldview is a direct reflection of the fact that half of our primary religious teachers and leaders do not have one. In some denominations, the vast majority of clergy do not have a biblical worldview, and it shows up clearly in the data related to the theological views and moral choices of people who attend those churches."[253]

8. The Last Days Will Be Terrible Times

Another sign of the last days is that they will be dangerous times. Second Timothy 3:1-4 warns, "Mark this: There will be terrible times in the last days. People will be lovers of themselves, lovers of money, boastful, proud, abusive, disobedient to their parents, ungrateful, unholy, without love, unforgiving, slanderous, without self-control, brutal, not lovers of the good, treacherous, rash, conceited, lovers of pleasure rather than lovers of God."

While statistics could be given for each of the above areas, a glimpse at only one of the above social evils communicates part of the scope of the problems we face today. Recent research on domestic abuse indicates, for instance, that...

- Estimates range from 960,000 incidents of violence against a current or former spouse, boyfriend, or girlfriend per year to three million women who are physically abused by their husband or boyfriend per year.

- Around the world, at least one in every three women has been beaten, coerced into sex or otherwise abused during her lifetime.

- Nearly one-third of American women (31 percent) report being physically or sexually abused by a husband or boyfriend at some point in their lives, according to a 1998 Commonwealth Fund survey.

- Nearly 25 percent of American women report being raped and/or physically assaulted by a current or former spouse, cohabiting partner, or date at some time in their lifetime.

- Thirty percent of Americans say they know a woman who has been physically abused by her husband or boyfriend in the past year.[254]

Unfortunately, this is only *one of eighteen* problem areas Paul mentions in 2 Timothy 3:1-4. Though ungodly behavior has always existed, it is clearly on the increase. This could easily fit Paul's statement about "terrible times in the last days."

9. People Will Abandon the True Christian Faith

Jesus warned, "Many will come in my name, claiming, 'I am the Christ,' and will deceive many" (Matthew 24:5). He also said, "Watch out for false prophets. They come to you in sheep's clothing, but inwardly they are ferocious wolves" (Matthew 7:15).

The apostle John wrote, "Dear children, this is the last hour; and as you have heard that the antichrist is coming, even now many antichrists have come. This is how we know it is the last hour" (1 John 2:18). And Paul said, "For such are false apostles, deceitful workers, transforming themselves into the apostles of Christ."

Many people today simply believe that everyone who talks about God is talking about the same God. In an interview, Dr. Ergun Caner shared an amazing comparison of the beliefs of Islam and Mormonism.

"We always get this in churches—'Oh, well, you know, it's the same God.' The easiest way that anyone can teach and explain what Islam basically is, is that it's medieval Mormonism. Everything that Joseph Smith did in the nineteenth century, Muhammad did in the seventh and eighth centuries. Everything that Islam developed was later copied.

"Think of it. First, they [both religions' founders] said that all the world was corrupt, that Christianity was corrupt, and there was no true religion on the planet when they came. Joseph Smith said this; Muhammad said this. Both of them said they received a revelation from an angel—Moroni (Mormonism), or Angel Jibrael (Muhammad). Both said they received the revelation from tablets—golden tablets. Both of them are preserved. The plates are buried in

Mormonism, and they are in heaven in Islam. Both of them taught that Judaism was true but lost it, that Christianity was true but lost it, and now they were here as the final word. Both of them taught that Jesus was a prophet, but not God. Both of them taught that Jesus said He would send a final prophet. In Mormonism it's Joseph Smith, in Islam it's Muhammad. Both of them taught that salvation is all works. Both of them have Jesus as a celestial brother, but not God in any sense. Both of them teach that women, in eternity, will be sexual servants. In Islam a woman is a *huriis.* In Mormonism she's eternally pregnant, a celestial bride."

10. People Will Doubt the Second Coming

Peter taught that in the last days, many will deny the return of Jesus Christ: "You must understand that in the last days scoffers will come, scoffing and following their own evil desires. They will say, 'Where is this "coming" he promised? Ever since our fathers died, everything goes on as it has since the beginning of creation'" (2 Peter 3:3-4).

When the film release of Tim LaHaye and Jerry Jenkins's *Left Behind* novel released in 2000, *Christianity Today's* film forum made a startling statement:

> Michael G. Maudlin, executive director of editorial operations for Christianity Today International, says on Beliefnet that while the movie is "pretty good," it's questionable to heavily promote the rapture as a core Christian belief. "This particular end-times scenario is only a hundred years old and theologically embraced by only a minority of evangelicalism's professional theologians and Bible scholars.... Most lay evangelicals think of the rapture, because of its savvy media saturation, as a doctrine as old and as sacrosanct as the Trinity."[255]

In other words, the review seemed to indicate that the rapture of Christians by Christ should not be presented as a core Christian belief. And such thinking will become common, according to Peter. Many will question whether Christ is returning at all, or at least question His imminent return.[256]

Yet Peter himself explains Christ's reason for waiting: "The Lord is not slow in keeping his promise, as some understand slowness. He is patient with you, not wanting anyone to perish, but everyone to come to repentance."[257] His delay is for people's benefit, not because of His negligence.

In summary, the Bible reveals several signs that will serve as indicators of the last days. While no one knows the time of Christ's return for certain, we cannot help but observe that all the signs discussed in this chapter are evident as growing trends in today's world.

18

All About the Rapture

"Wherever this truth [the Rapture] has been taught, it has had the same effect on believers that it had in the first three centuries—it produced holy living in an unholy age, a drive for evangelism, and a zeal for missions."[258]

DR. TIM LAHAYE

Over the past 25 years, I (John) have served as a plenary speaker at over 30 prophecy conferences. I've learned what people value most, what they respond to, and where people are on the issues. I've also discovered that one of the names people have responded to the most on the subject of the rapture is the late Dr. John Walvoord.

Dr. John Walvoord was a professor at Dallas Theological Seminary for over 60 years, serving an amazing 34 years as its president. He was also the author of more than 30 books, including several best-sellers. He was a keynote speaker at top Bible prophecy events nationwide for over five decades. Those who held different views on prophecy would even invite him to speak at their conferences because he did not argue with them. He simply came and presented his view. His death in 2002 ended an enormous swath of biblical materials on the end times, especially resources on the important issue of the rapture.

In June 1993, a few years before Dr. Walvoord's death, I had the privilege of sitting with him for five hours for a series of television programs to unearth the treasures of his numerous years of research on the imminent, any-moment return of Jesus Christ. In contrast with some of the high-pressure, sensationalist, date-setting

personalities who spoke on this
topic, I found Dr. Walvoord a kind,
endearing gentleman who exuded an
unmatched passion to share what the
Scriptures teach about the rapture.

The Hope of the Rapture

As we began, Dr. Walvoord spoke
of his own personal excitement at
the prospect of seeing Jesus face to
face. "I've been teaching prophecy
for more than fifty years at the seminary level. It's a very precious truth
and a very practical one, but it's more
than just a doctrine to me. The idea of
being able to see Christ perhaps any
day, face to face, is an amazing, electrifying anticipation. I believe
that's what the Bible teaches and I believe that's what God wants us
to realize and to hope for."

The Problems in Understanding the Rapture

Dr. Walvoord turned from excitement to disappointment as he
described the major problem with teaching prophecy in the church
today. "Though we can deal with this subject from a theological,
biblical standpoint, if you also deal with it from the standpoint that
you really love Christ, you're going to love [the anticipation of] His
appearing, and this is going to be a precious truth to you. The major
problem in prophecy is that there is almost universal ignorance on
the subject because it isn't taught in many churches."

Dr. Walvoord launched into a story regarding the Southern Baptist spiritual giant and personal friend Dr. W.A. Criswell, the late
pastor of First Baptist Church of Dallas to illustrate his point.[260] "I
was in a large Baptist church and Dr. Criswell and I were sharing this
conference. The pastor introduced me by saying he had graduated
from a well-recognized theological seminary, received a master's

degree in theology, and *didn't hear one lecture on biblical prophecy.* He said, 'I'm here to learn like the rest of you.'

"Obviously, pastors who haven't had any training in this field don't know what to do with it and aren't going to preach it. The result is that many churches are totally ignorant on this subject. There are other reasons prophecy isn't taught, such as the fact that it's so confusing. I was in one church at the pastor's invitation and I asked him if he preached on prophecy. 'Oh no,' he said. 'I can't. I don't know enough.'

"I asked another pastor of a church that believed in the rapture as a part of their doctrinal beliefs why he never preached on prophecy. He said, 'It's too technical. It's too controversial.' So he avoided the subject completely. Yet that's *not* what the Bible does. About one-fourth of the Bible was prophetic when it was given, and about half of these promises have already been literally fulfilled."

Dr. Walvoord further agonized over the great confusion churches have over the matter of prophecy. "There are so many different views. For an ordinary person trying to study this subject, it's very bewildering. Even scholars struggle with the fact there are multiple views of prophecy. There's a reason for it. I once asked myself, 'Why is there this confusion?' I've discovered it's because the prophecies that lead up to and follow the second coming aren't always interpreted literally. This stems from a movement in the church way back in the third century when the school at Alexandria, Egypt took the position that the Bible could not be interpreted literally. The Bible was considered just one grand metaphor.

"I think that is absolutely false! I had the challenge of producing a book that interpreted every prophecy in the Bible, entitled *The Prophecy Knowledge Handbook.* It's an 800-page book in which I started in Genesis and moved all the way through the whole Bible. As I did so, I thought, *How in the world can I work my way through all these conflicting opinions?* I chose a very simple solution. I asked myself in each case, What does the prophecy *teach?* What does it *mean?* I found if you followed that simple formula, you could fit together all the prophecies of the Bible without contradiction and get a complete picture of not only prophecy fulfilled but prophecy *to be fulfilled* in the future."

The Uniqueness of the Rapture

Dr. Walvoord then opened his well-worn leather Bible. "The confusion that takes place in studying prophecy often comes from a lack of attention to what the Bible actually says. The rapture—Christ coming for His own—is a very particular doctrine. It predicts that Christ is going to cause dead Christians to be resurrected and Christians who are alive to be instantly changed to rise from the earth and meet the Lord in the air and enter heaven.

"Now, there's only *one* rapture. There are many *resurrections* in the Bible, but only one rapture. Christ introduced this truth for the very first time in John 14 when His disciples were struggling with His announcement that He was going to leave."

As Dr. Walvoord continued to talk about the rapture, he increased his pace. Flipping quickly to the appropriate page in his Bible, he said, "In John 14:3, Jesus said, 'If I go and prepare a place for you, I will come again, and receive you unto myself, that where I am, there ye may be also' [KJV]. This fell on absolutely deaf ears because the disciples were confused about there being two separate comings. Everybody was confused in the Old Testament and in the Gospels. They put the first and second comings of Christ together as if they were one event and thought that in His first coming, He was going to fulfill the promises relating to His second coming. Now Jesus introduces this additional element. He's going to *come and take them* to heaven. This wasn't their view at all. They were looking for a kingdom on earth. So Jesus introduced the rapture here, and later on, Paul gives us a further exposition on it."

The Bible on the Rapture

I asked Dr. Walvoord to provide a few more specifics on the rapture. He said, "When it comes to the doctrine of the rapture, what does the Bible actually teach? Christ predicted the rapture in John 14, but it wasn't until later that the apostle Paul taught about the rapture, in his letter to the Thessalonians. Paul had been at the Thessalonian church for three weeks and preached the gospel, including the fact that Christ was coming. Then he was forced to leave because of opposition and threats on his life. He sent Timothy back to see how the people were getting along, and Timothy came back to Paul with questions from them.

"The Thessalonians knew that Christ was coming for them, but what about their dead loved ones? Timothy couldn't answer that question. The Thessalonians also didn't know *when* they would be raised. It wasn't until Paul wrote his first letter to this church that he gave a clear account of how the dead are going to be raised and how the living are going to be taken into heaven.

"In 1 Thessalonians 4:13, Paul gives us this revelation: 'I would not have you to be ignorant, brethren, concerning them which are asleep, that ye sorrow not, even as others which have no hope' [KJV]. Here Paul makes clear that God doesn't want us to be ignorant but wants us to *know* what prophecy teaches. He wants us to know because this gives us a real hope that the world doesn't have. In other words, we can anticipate the wonderful return of Christ.

"Then in verse 14 Paul states the certainty of it: 'If we believe that Jesus died and rose again, even so them also which sleep in Jesus will God bring with him' [KJV]. Now the resurrection of Christ is mentioned in Old Testament prophecy. By the time Paul wrote this letter, it had already been fulfilled. It had taken place. What Paul is telling us is that the rapture is just as certain as the resurrection of Christ, even though the rapture had not yet been fulfilled. He tells us this promise will be fulfilled.

"Then he tells us that when the rapture occurs, God will bring with Him those who sleep in Jesus. In other words, those who have died in the Christian faith are going to be brought back to the earth at the time of the rapture. Why? Their bodies are going to be resurrected from the grave and their souls will reenter their bodies. He goes on to tell us in the verses that follow:

> This we say unto you by the word of the Lord, that we which are alive and remain unto the coming of the Lord shall not prevent them which are asleep. For the Lord himself shall descend from heaven with a shout, with the voice of the archangel, and with the trump of God: and the dead in Christ shall rise first: then we which are alive and remain

shall be caught up [raptured] together with them in the clouds, to meet the Lord in the air: and so shall we ever be with the Lord [KJV].

"This passage gives us the great truths of the rapture of the church."

Details About the Rapture

Clearly, Dr. Walvoord was in his element. His summaries of a lifetime of scholarship and personal study were revealed through the perspiration on his brow as he leaned downward so his eyes could adjust as he peered through his thick-rimmed glasses at the Scriptures. Most people at this point would be exhausted, but Dr. Walvoord appeared to be exhilarated.

"Notice the details that Paul gives us about the rapture. First, the Lord is going to descend physically from heaven to the earth. This is an important event. He actually comes in the air. He will not touch the Earth. He says people will hear the voice of the archangel and the trumpet of God. This is literally a shout of command. Christians who have died will be resurrected, and Christians who are still alive will be translated and given bodies suitable for heaven. It is those Christians who are alive who will be 'caught up.' That's where we get the word *rapture*. We will meet the Lord in the air and we will always be with the Lord…. If we're alive, we will be changed instantly. If we're dead, we'll be raised from the dead and we'll meet the Lord in the air and then proceed to heaven."

The Results of the Rapture

Switching to a different portion of the New Testament, Dr. Walvoord noted another passage in which the apostle Paul comments on the rapture. "In 1 Corinthians 15, Paul is dealing with the subject of the resurrection and this matter of the rapture of the church. Beginning in verse 51, he shares these wonderful truths:

Behold, I show you a mystery; we shall not all sleep, but we shall all be changed, in a moment, in the twinkling of an eye,

at the last trump: for the trumpet shall sound, and the dead
will be raised incorruptible, and we shall be changed. For
this corruptible must put on incorruption, and this mortal
must put on immortality [KJV].

"Those of us who are alive as Christians today recognize we have
some problems. First, we have a body that is given to us by our parents, and it's a sinful body. It's able to sin. In fact, every Christian
sins. It's also a body that grows older. Whether you resist it or not,
eventually you grow older. Finally, it's mortal. That is, it can die." As
Walvoord spoke, I remembered the fact that his health was failing
and I knew that he felt the impact of these words personally.

He continued, with great passion, "Now, these three things have
to be changed. I believe when the rapture occurs, we are going to
be changed instantly and we will be given bodies patterned after the
resurrection body of Christ. This will make us suitable for being in
the Lord's presence in heaven. We couldn't stand to be in the presence of a holy God in our present bodies. So a whole generation of
Christians could go to heaven without dying.

"In the Old Testament, both Enoch and Elijah went to heaven
without dying, but they're the only exceptions. Everybody else who
ever lived has died. But someday there will be a whole generation
that's going to be changed rather than die. This is our wonderful
prospect. Whether we're young Christians, middle-aged, or older,
we have this wonderful hope that when Christ comes, and that could
happen any day, we'll be raptured and our bodies will be changed
instantly."

Wrapping Up the Rapture

As I closed this interview, I asked Dr. Walvoord for some final
thoughts for people just beginning to learn about the rapture. He
gave a very direct response: "For some of you this may be new.
The truth of the Lord's coming is a very wonderful truth because it
teaches us that our prospect of going to heaven is not some distant
thing that may come after suffering and death, but it could be today.
It's a *comfort*."

On December 22, 2002, Dr. Walvoord passed away at the age of 92. Choosing a small, private funeral, his family gathered to pay their last respects. Dallas Seminary president Dr. Mark Bailey commented in the *Dallas Morning News* obituary, "He's really one of the heroes of our faith. He has been absolutely faithful to his calling, his wife and his family. He's been a man of integrity, free of scandal, with impeccable morals and ethics. It's a rare commodity these days."[261]

Marked by a life of integrity and a tremendous influence around the globe, Dr. Walvoord ended his life ready to meet his Maker. I (Dillon) still remember my graduation from Dallas Seminary in 2002, only months before Dr. Walvoord's death. As a gift, each graduate was given a copy of Dr. Walvoord's biography, each personally signed by him. Over 300 times he signed his name as an encouragement to future Christian leaders. When I spoke with other Dallas Seminary leaders, I learned this was the norm for John Walvoord. He personally signed thousands of letters and books, praying for the recipient of each one, and encouraging those who follow Christ to pursue Him fully.

This was his lifestyle, his attitude. Now he is experiencing what he anticipated all of his life: "The idea of being able to see Christ perhaps any day, face to face, is an amazing, electrifying anticipation."[262]

19

What Happens After the Rapture?

*"What would you say if the headline tomorrow morning is:
'Here's a new idea. We'll let the Israelis have their temple
worship. An amazing suggestion has come up.
We can move the Dome of the Rock lovingly, carefully,
to Mecca, and by the way, the Israelis said they're a little
uncomfortable. They would sign [a peace treaty] for seven
years.' That's the ball game."*[263]

DR. ZOLA LEVITT

*"Now, for the first time in 2000 years, we see Jews. Maybe
it's a minority, maybe it's a handful of Jews, but that
minority can be a very vocal and demonstrable minority.
They are preparing to rebuild the temple."*[264]

DR. RANDALL PRICE

At a hotel conference center near the Dallas-Fort Worth International Airport, I (John) had finally finished preparing, with my team, the set for our live recording on Bible prophecy. We were at one of the best hotels in the nation, with the best taping equipment of the time, and the ballroom was packed with people seeking information on the end times from the top prophecy experts in the world. We had flown in several of them from across the United States, Canada, and Israel. Combined, these scholars had written dozens of books on prophecy and spoken to hundreds of thousands of people around the world. It was an honor to stand among these spiritual giants as they conversed with one another and my audience and drew an intense level of interest from every viewer.

A major focus of our time together was the sequence of events that will take place following the rapture. These events include the seven-year period the Bible calls the Tribulation—a time during which a future world political leader called the Antichrist will rise, and ultimately, will be destroyed when Christ returns to establish His kingdom on earth. The views taught by these prophecy experts may be controversial to some. However, the goal here is to present the best of our recording, allowing *you* to evaluate the evidence and decide for yourself what the Bible says about these last-days events.

What Is the Tribulation?

Dr. David Breese, a towering intellectual with an incredible mastery of words, helped to provide a clear definition of the Tribulation. With intense fervor, he said, "The Bible teaches that Christ is coming at the end of the age—that's at the end of the Tribulation—in power and great glory. He's coming with ten thousands of His saints. That great announcement of history will be when He establishes His kingdom.

"The Scriptures teach that preceding that glorious return of Christ will be a seven-year period called the Tribulation. It's about the Tribulation that the Scripture says to Christians: 'Because you have kept the word of My perseverance, *I also will keep you from the hour of testing* [or tribulation] which is about to come upon the whole world, to test those who dwell on the earth' [NASB].[265]

"Therefore, we see in Scripture that the Bible says that Christ will come for His saints *before* the beginning of the Tribulation and take all believing Christians up to be with Him in heaven. So we can assure every believer that there's coming a moment when they will be caught up in their physical bodies into the presence of Jesus Christ to be with the Lord forever. Perhaps, in short, we might say that Christ is coming at the end of the Tribulation *with* His saints, but before that He is coming *for* His saints. When the rapture comes and Christians are taken out of the world, instantly the salt of the earth is gone. He is going to take us, the bride of Christ, out before that day."

The Four Horsemen of the Apocalypse

A significant aspect of the Tribulation is the four horsemen of the apocalypse. Seen in everything from the *X-Files, Charmed,* Clint Eastwood's *Pale Rider, Tombstone,* and even episodes of *The Simpsons* and *South Park,* the idea of four scary horses and their riders has captured the attention of our culture.[266] Commenting on the biblical account, Dr. Breese noted, "The advent of the Tribulation is one of the most spectacular passages in Scripture. The horsemen of the apocalypse appear like a cavalry charge. It would have been the most frightening experience of the old days: the white horse, the red horse, the black horse, and then the pale horse.

"At the advent of the pale horse, one-fourth of the population of the world is killed. Two chapters later in Revelation 9, one-third of the remainder are killed. So we know that one-half of the population of the world will die during the Tribulation. This is compounded by the rise of Antichrist, stars falling from heaven, wormwood that makes the water undrinkable, and other fearful events. For instance, Revelation 6 tells about an earthquake and then says that the chief captains and the mighty men and the great men will cry out to the mountains and the rocks and say, 'Fall on us and hide us from the face of him who sits on the throne and from the wrath of the Lamb!' [verse 16]. It is not to be contemplated lightly."

Daniel's 70 Weeks

Switching the topic to the ancient Jewish prophet Daniel, I asked Dr. Zola Levitt, a Christian of Jewish background known for taping many of his programs on location in Israel, to comment on the mysterious "70 weeks" of Daniel. His response helped those of us not from Israel to better understand the cultural implications of Daniel's prophecies.

"All prophecy is about the Jews and it all happens in Israel. As the nations go back and forth with Israel in war and commerce, then they are mentioned. But it is really *Jewish* prophecy. The Bible is a Jewish book primarily written and published in Israel.

"The angel said in Daniel 9:24-27 that 'seventy weeks are determined upon thy people' [KJV]. So we have a figure. 'Weeks,' in Hebrew, can indicate sets of seven years. If you do the arithmetic, you could check Daniel. He was right. The Messiah indeed came and was cut off; but in sixty-nine weeks. It left seven years yet to go. Comparing Daniel to Revelation 11 and other passages, we see that these final seven years are clearly the Tribulation.

"This prophecy will be fulfilled and that seventieth week will be determined on Israel. It's about the Antichrist making a covenant with Israel. It's about the Antichrist stopping the sacrifices and the offerings. It's about the Antichrist going into the temple in Jerusalem and saying he is the God of Israel. It's about the gathering storm at Armageddon."

The Purpose of Tribulation

One of our other panelists provided an intriguing picture of the

DOES IT ADD UP?

According to Dr. Allen Ross, who holds a ThD from Dallas Seminary and a PhD from Cambridge University,

> It is a matter of mathematics: 69 weeks times seven years times 360 days [lunar calendar] will give us the number of days in the prophecy: 173,880 days. So Daniel is saying after the decree of March 5, 444 B.C., there are 173,880 days until Messiah is cut off.

> Now, this can be verified with our calendar system. The difference between 444 B.C. and 33 A.D. is 476 solar years. How many days is that? By multiplying 476 by 365.24219879 (or by 365 days, 5 hours, 48 minutes, 45.975 seconds), one gets 173,855 days, 6 hours, 52 minutes, 44 seconds—or 173,855 days. There is a difference of 25 days. But the solar reckoning is from March 5, 444 to March 5, 32 A.D. So if we add the difference of the 25 days to March 5, we come to March 30 (of A.D. 33), which in the year 33 A.D. was Nisan 10. That is the Monday of the Passion Week, the day of the Triumphal entry of Jesus into Jerusalem. Jesus died Nisan 14, 33 A.D., or April 3, 33 A.D.

Dr. Allen Ross, "Messianic Prophecies,"
Biblical Studies Foundation.[267]

Tribulation's purpose, sharing, "If you take a look at Daniel 9, you will have reference to what will take place by the end of those 490 years. The time of peace comes in; Israel accepts their Messiah; the birth of the millennial period, the kingdom time. Before the end of the Tribulation period, this seven years finds Israel surrounded by all the nations of the earth, gathered around to finally push Israel into the sea, push this last reminder of God right off the face of the earth so man can finally find his own new world without God. In the process, they meet not only Israel but the Lord Himself, who comes to rescue Israel.

"Scripture says, 'In that day.... they shall look upon Me whom they have pierced' [KJV]. [268] They recognize Him as the Messiah. The 490 years of Daniel 9 is fulfilled on that day, and we have the birth of the millennial kingdom, fulfilling all that was written 2,500 years ago."

Faith in the Tribulation?

Second Thessalonians 2 says the Antichrist will come upon the world scene in the end times. Verse 6 tells us that in this time, the "restrainer" (Holy Spirit) will be removed. This leads to an intriguing question: How will people be drawn to Christ during the Tribulation if the Holy Spirit is removed? Dr. Randall Price's words offered a balanced and encouraging answer:

"I think the first thing to note is that those who were in the church at Thessalonica were quite concerned about whether they were already in that Tribulation period. Since they had the Holy Spirit, how could it be that the Day of the Lord had come? He says the reason they should not think this is the Tribulation happening is because the Holy Spirit is still present in the world, restraining the world order, so that the events described in the Tribulation don't break out.

"During the Tribulation the Holy Spirit will still be *in the world*, but He won't be *within the church*. That's the point of that passage. The church will be removed, with its presence of the Holy Spirit, before that day comes. The Holy Spirit will still be there in that time just as He was in the Old Testament—and will still be able to draw people to Himself because the Lord's presence will be there. That's why we have those great witnesses that come during the Tribulation period, even the 144,000 who are sealed to carry on that testimony. People will still be saved in the energy of the Holy Spirit."

What About the Antichrist?

It's nearly impossible to talk about the end times without mentioning the Antichrist. One of our experts noted, "He's going to be the greatest charismatic leader that the world has ever seen. He will be built perfectly for the media age in which we live today. He is going to be the leader that seemingly will bring us toward the long-awaited world peace and deceive the world into believing he is Christ. I believe he is going to deceive Israel into believing he is the Messiah who has finally brought peace to this part of the world where *shalom,* peace, has long been wanted."

But who will the Antichrist target? Dr. Levitt remarked, "Israel is a *particular target* of the Antichrist. This is the final triumph of anti-Semitism, of which we are now seeing plenty of signs, including famine, pestilence, and earthquakes. The Antichrist will stumble on Israel." While the specifics of this intriguing character presented by the apostle John in the book of Revelation are not clearly given, the Bible does indicate a world leader will arise who will deceive the nations and claim the allegiance of all during the seven-year Tribulation by means of the controversial mark of the beast.

The Mark of the Beast

As one of our experts explained, "The phrase itself is telling. It is *the* mark of *the* beast. We have talked about the beast a great deal, this great Antichrist who arises onto the scene. But we have to recognize the world in which the Antichrist arises. First, the rapture has taken place. Millions of people have vanished off the face of the Earth.

"What is that going to do to the world left behind? Millions of people are suddenly gone. People have watched family members disappear. Children have vanished. It is going to drive the world insane. News networks will go to immediate worldwide coverage. You know that people will be glued to their televisions, trying to figure out what has taken place. There will be chaos and confusion.

"God Himself will send a strong delusion upon the world. As the people are viewing their television sets in this moment of panic, someone will come before them. He is this Antichrist. The Bible tells us the first words that come out of his mouth in Revelation 13:6: 'He opened his mouth to blaspheme God.'

"So immediately you have someone standing up, saying, 'Where is this God you've heard about? It's time for us to recognize the power that's *within* us. It's time for us to forget about a new heavens and a new earth and build a new age on *this* earth. Let's build our own kingdom *right here*. Let's forget all this God stuff. Everybody who's on my side, let's take this mark of unity.' The same chapter says that without this mark, nobody will be able to buy or sell anything.

"But it's not primarily about buying and selling. It's about allegiance. It's the pride of mankind. The mark of the beast is simply the mark that people take to say, 'Hey, I believe this thing.' And at the same time, they're saying, 'I don't believe God.'"

A Final Peace

As we transitioned to the ultimate peace Israel seeks and only Christ can bring, Dr. Levitt recounted an amazing story. "When I went to Israel to make TV programs, I wanted to make programs about how God had given this land to Israel. 'Israel, by Divine Right' was the name of the series. I traveled to Shechem, where God gave the land to Abraham, and to Bethel, where God came to Jacob in a dream and they anointed a stone.

"For the first time in my life I carried a .9 millimeter pistol in my shirt. I don't even know how to use a gun! It was considered a 'good negotiating position.' But imagine me going to my own land having to carry this thing because it was dangerous. Every member of the crew was armed. We had security guys pretending to be TV crew members. This is why peace is such a huge deal for Israel."

At the end of the panel discussion, I asked Dr. Breese to summarize the Tribulation, offering some perspective to the issues we had discussed. His words are still some of the best I've ever heard for communicating a complex matter in a succinct way. With a serious tone, he said, "The Tribulation sees the rise of Antichrist, and the establishment of world government and world religion. Then the Antichrist decides that the irritant to his total power is this faint memory of the existence of God as represented by Jerusalem, Israel. So he initiates a global war against Israel, and that war, interestingly enough, is concluded by a rescue from heaven. The sky opens up, and a mighty army comes down from heaven.

"John describes this in Revelation 19, saying, 'I saw heaven standing open and there before me was a white horse, whose rider is called Faithful and True.' And we are told 'the armies of heaven were following him.' When Jesus comes in His glorious return, we are coming back with Him. I'm not sure how many horseback riders we have in the crowd today, but everybody should learn to ride because we will be part of that returning and victorious army."

The rapture will be a time of celebration for many; it will be a time of utter chaos for many others. According to our prophecy experts, the days following the rapture will see a leader declaring world peace, yet this same leader will usher in the worst times the Earth has ever seen. He will lead a final effort to destroy Israel, and God will bring a rescue from heaven. Then the Messiah will begin His earthly reign, and ultimately, a new heavens and Earth will be created for those who know Christ and will live with Him forever.

Yet a few questions remain. Does America have a part in Bible prophecy? What ultimately happens to Israel? And how can we know for certain our eternal destiny? These are our topics in the chapters that remain.

20

Where Is America in Bible Prophecy?

*"One of the hardest things for American prophecy
students to accept is that the United States is not clearly
mentioned in Bible prophecy, yet our nation is the
only superpower in the world today."*[269]

DR. TIM LAHAYE

While America is never directly mentioned in the Bible's prophecies, there have been many attempts to find it:

> Some believe that America is the unnamed nation in Isaiah 18. Others believe that "the young lions of Tarshish" in Ezekiel 38:13 is a veiled reference to America. Still others maintain that America, or New York City, is Babylon the Great, the great prostitute city, in Revelation 17–18.[270]

Most prophecy scholars agree that the United States is never clearly mentioned in the prophecies of the Old or New Testaments. But why? What explains this scriptural silence? Dr. Tim LaHaye, prophecy scholar and coauthor of the *Left Behind*® series, has noted:

> "Does the United States have a place in end time prophecy?" My first response is no, there is nothing about the U.S. in prophecy! At least nothing that is specific. There is an allusion to a group of nations in Ezekiel 38:13 that could apply, but even that is not specific. The question is *why?* Why would the God of prophecy not refer to the supreme superpower nation in the end times in preparation for the one-world government of the Antichrist?[271]

Possible Explanations Regarding America

Dr. Mark Hitchcock, author of *Is America in Bible Prophecy?* provides four possible explanations for why America is not mentioned in the Bible's prophetic teachings. During a recent interview, Dr. Hitchcock and I (Dillon) explored these four viewpoints.[272]

1. America Will Remain Strong, but Unmentioned

Most nations of the modern world are not mentioned directly in the Bible. America could be one of them. According to this view, just because America is a superpower does not necessarily indicate we must somehow be in the Bible. In the grand scheme of history, the United States, as a country, is less than 250 years old—much younger than the nations that are discussed in biblical prophecy.

According to Dr. Hitchcock, this answer is possible but seems unlikely. In Scripture, the dominant political and military power in the end times is centered in the Mediterranean and Europe. This scriptural silence concerning America seems to indicate that by the time the Tribulation period arrives, America will no longer be a major influence in the world.

In addition, America serves as the most noted ally of Israel among Western nations. Wouldn't the Bible at least indirectly mention America if this alliance remains during the end times? Though God could choose to simply keep silent about America, this doesn't seem a likely option.

2. America Will Be Weakened from Attack by Outside Forces

This disturbing option says that America will somehow lose its political, economic, and military influence before the arrival of the end times. Those who hold to this theory are quick to point to the notion that America could be crippled by a nuclear attack. Considering the events of 9/11, the nuclear development taking place in anti-American nations, and the increasing amount of terrorism in today's world, this is certainly possible.

Harvard professor Dr. Graham Allison's book *Nuclear Terrorism* notes that given current circumstances, a nuclear attack on America within the next ten years is "more likely than not."[273] President George W. Bush has called nuclear terrorism the single most serious threat to American national security.

In a 2003 poll, 40 percent of Americans said they worry often about the chances of a nuclear attack by terrorists.[274] The fear exists, the potential is real, and it *could* be the reason for America's absence in end-times prophecy.

3. America Will Have Lost Her Influence from Decay

This view has become very popular due to the tremendous amount of moral decay shown in daily newspapers, television shows, and online publications. High divorce rates, overcrowded prisons, sexual promiscuity, gambling addictions, alcohol and drug abuse, domestic violence, and homicide, along with increased levels of violence and sexuality portrayed in today's films, television, and video games, cause many to argue that America's lack of prominence in the end times results from its own moral demise.

Again, this is possible, but there is another perspective that indicates a more likely scenario, according to Dr. Hitchcock.

4. America Is Weakened Due to the Rapture

If the rapture were to happen today and all the true believers in Jesus Christ disappeared to heaven in a single moment, America as we know it could be obliterated. It is estimated that America will lose somewhere between 25 to 65 million citizens—Christians and their small children.[275] Not only would the country lose a minimum of 10 percent of her population, but she would also lose the very best, the "salt and light"[276] of the nation.

Prophecy expert Dr. Charles Dyer estimates the number at approximately 28 million Americans, and writes,

> Can you imagine the effects on our country if over 28 million people…disappear? That is approximately double the entire population of New York City, Los Angeles, Chicago, and Houston all rolled together!… America could not support an army in the Middle East because the military would be needed at home to control the chaos![277]

According to Dr. Hitchcock, what makes the most sense is that America will suffer a great fall due to the rapture, then possibly join forces with Europe as it becomes the dominant world government.

What Does This Mean?

Will America suddenly collapse due to nuclear attack, terrorist action, economic depression, or rampant immorality? No one knows for sure. While these options are possible, only God knows America's future as a nation. What appears certain regarding America's future role is this:

- America is not specifically mentioned in end-times Bible prophecy;

- America does not hold a prominent role in the Tribulation period (unless it is included as part of the one-world government); and

- America will change dramatically upon the occurrence of the rapture.

For all Americans, these factors should serve as a call to humility and personal spiritual reflection. American pride must be countered with a humble acknowledgment of God's power and plans for our lives and the future. In addition, in light of the Bible's past accuracy and future predictions, we must personally evaluate our relationship with God, taking the necessary spiritual steps to prepare both for our personal afterlife and the end times.

21

What Is Israel's Future?

*"The most important reason Jews and Arabs cannot get
together is not land…it is not money or history.
The reason for the continual conflict over the city of
Jerusalem is theology."*[278]

JOHN HAGEE, IN *JERUSALEM COUNTDOWN*

Ultimately the War on Terror has *spiritual* rather than political roots.

Dr. William Varner, professor of biblical studies at The Master's College in Santa Clarita, California, holds a doctorate from Temple University, a master's degree in Jewish Studies from Dropsie College, and has also directed The Master's College study program in Israel. He has contributed to the Ankerberg Theological Research Institute for years, both to the theological journal and its online database of research articles.

His wealth of knowledge has developed the minds of prophecy students for decades. Based on his biblical and historical expertise on the nation of Israel, he concludes that the future of the Jewish people rests on two fundamental foundations: the physical restoration of Israel, and the divine promises to Israel.[279]

The Physical Restoration of Israel

*"I will take you out of the nations; I will gather you from all
the countries and bring you into your own land."*

EZEKIEL 36:24

Dr. Varner notes that in the context of Ezekiel chapter 36, God is declaring that the exile of Israel has come about because of the people's sin and idol worship (36:16-19). The punishment for this would be exile among the nations of the world. After a partial return from the Babylonian exile in 536 B.C., Israel later experienced a second stage of that exile in A.D. 70 with the fall of Jerusalem and the temple. During the last 2,000 years, the Jewish people have literally been scattered to the ends of the earth. In those countries of exile, they would even give cause for the Gentiles to blaspheme God's name because of their condition (36:20-33). In other words, when people see "the LORD's people" (verse 20) in such pitiful condition, there will be some scoffers who mockingly declare that these people who had been chosen by the Lord are now profaning His name by their condition.

This raises an interesting problem that God Himself anticipates— a problem to which He Himself offers the solution. How will the Master of the Universe restore the honor of His tarnished name? How will He prove to the nations that He exists and that He is not untrue to His word? He will do this by reversing the Jewish exile and removing the stain and shame of the *Diaspora,* or Dispersion.

Nothing could be clearer than the three steps God promises in verse 24. The three verbs are active: "take you," "gather you," "bring you." The scattered Jewish exiles will be taken and gathered from the many nations to which they were dispersed. They will then be brought back together to the land of origin—"your own land"—the land of Abraham, Isaac, and Jacob. Heading God's future program will be the restored nation of Israel.

Just over 100 years ago there was a tiny community of Jews living in the Turkish backwater called Palestine. They were poor, living mostly on donations from their fellow Jews abroad. Anything like a "return to Zion" was viewed by most theologians, Christian and Jewish, as an extremely unlikely possibility. But a century of intensive immigration, settlement, sacrifice, toil, and wars for their lives has led to the founding of a nation with one of the world's strongest armies and most technologically advanced societies.

Secular historians such as Arnold Toynbee,[280] for example, cannot explain the reason for this amazing restoration. A people who were once exiled from their ancient homeland, losing both their land and even their ancient language, have been restored to both! Skeptics, on the other hand, will point either to luck or American support or some other human explanation for this unique phenomenon in the history of humanity.

The most surprising explanation, however, comes from some theologians who have factored out the divine promises to Israel and transferred them to the church. They point to the secular nature of Israel's society as evidence that God has nothing to do with this nation. They forget that Ezekiel also prophesied that the bones would come together without breath first, before the Spirit then blows upon them (37:1-14). In other words, there will be a restoration to the land (in unbelief) *before* there will be a restoration to the Lord.

It appears that the secular historians, unbelieving skeptics, and the spiritualizing theologians all refuse to admit and accept the only unbiased explanation. This explanation is grounded in the promises to Israel proclaimed through dozens of Old and New Testament prophets. That explanation is that the God who was responsible for the exile and who suffered the slander of His reputation during that exile is the same God who will honor His name by beginning the process of returning these wandering sons of Jacob to their homeland. He does this not because they deserve it, but because He is gracious, merciful, and faithful. Yes, Israel still stands in need of the Messiah, Jesus. But it is hard to explain away the evident force of so many biblical promises. Even in their unbelief, the regathered children of Israel are a testimony to God's faithfulness and to His promises.

The Divine Promises to Israel

The apostle Paul is clear on the great privileges that God has granted Israel. He wrote in Romans 9:4 that it is the "Israelites, to whom pertain the adoption, the glory, the covenants, the giving of the law, the service of God, and the promises" (NKJV). Paul nowhere hints that these great privileges have been annulled, forfeited, or cancelled. One of the purposes of the three chapters of which this verse is a part (Romans 9-11) is to emphasize that God has not cancelled

His promises to Israel or transferred them to some other people. Romans 11:1-2 tells us, "I say then, has God cast away His people? Certainly not! For I also am an Israelite, of the seed of Abraham, of the tribe of Benjamin. God has not cast away His people whom He foreknew" (NKJV).

Specifically, what are those promises to Israel? Well, they ultimately are derived from those given to "Father Abraham" in Genesis 12:1-3. To sum them up, they are:

- the promises of a people
- the promises of a land, and
- the promises of a blessing.

Deuteronomy also affirms these promises to Israel. Chapters 28–29 clearly outline the dire consequences if Israel disobeys the Lord. There will be drought, exile, suffering, and much more. Even if the promises of judgment are fulfilled, that does not cancel the promises of Israel's future blessings found in Deuteronomy 30.

One Old Testament example of this very principle can be seen in the life of the prophet Hosea. In Hosea 3:4 there is a promise of judgment on Israel that already has been literally fulfilled: "The children of Israel shall abide many days without king or prince, without sacrifice or sacred pillar, without ephod or teraphim" (NKJV). If that verse has had a literal fulfillment in Israel's history of the last 2,000 years, what about the next verse embodying a promise of blessing for Israel?: "Afterward the children of Israel shall return and seek the LORD their God and David their king. They shall fear the LORD and His goodness in the latter days" (NKJV). If Israel was punished literally, then it must be blessed literally!

Or consider the dual promises of judgment and blessing in Micah 3:12–4:2:

> Because of you Zion shall be plowed like a field, Jerusalem shall become heaps of ruins, and the mountain of the temple like the bare hills of the forest. Now it shall come to pass *in the latter days* that the mountain of the LORD's house shall be established on the top of the mountains, and shall be

exalted above the hills; and peoples shall flow to it. Many nations shall come and say, "Come, and let us go up to the mountain of the LORD, to the house of the God of Jacob; He will teach us His ways, and we shall walk in His paths." For out of Zion the law shall go forth, and the word of the LORD from Jerusalem (NKJV, emphasis added).

We know that the promise of the destruction of Jerusalem and the temple was fulfilled literally. Why would anyone then spiritualize the promise of restoration and blessing for Jerusalem and the temple in the very next verses?

Paul notes in his letter to the Romans, "All Israel will be saved, as it is written: 'The Deliverer will come out of Zion, and He will turn away ungodliness from Jacob; for this is My covenant with them, when I take away their sins'" (Romans 11:26-27 ESV). Paul clearly bases his theology of literal blessings for a literal Israel on Old Testament prophecies (Isaiah 59:20-21; Jeremiah 31:33-34).[281] As a result of God's literal promises to Israel, we can know *for sure* there is a lot of action still to take place in the Holy Land.

The words of the poet and novelist Robert Louis Stevenson provide a great admonition to those today willing to listen:

> I cannot understand how you theologians and preachers can apply to the church Scripture promises, which, in their plain meaning apply to God's chosen people, Israel; and which consequently must be future. The prophetic books are full of teachings which, if they are interpreted literally, would be inspiring, and a magnificent assurance of a great and glorious future; but which, as they are spiritualized, become farcical...as applied to the church they are a comedy.[282]

22

Making *Your* Future Certain

"If there ever was an hour when men should consider their personal relationship to Jesus Christ, it is today."[283]

DR. JOHN WALVOORD

In the midst of the Middle East meltdown and uncertainties in our world today, the God who rules over history makes some irrevocable promises, offering a hope and future that is certain. God wants to have a personal relationship with you *now.* He wants to free you from the guilt and issues in your life *now,* no matter who you are or what you have done.

As we approach the end of our journey together on this issue of the Middle East meltdown, would you allow us the opportunity to ask seven vital questions regarding your personal future? We hope and pray that your answers will assist in further preparing you for life in this world and in the next.

In the darkness of the night, as people reflect back on the activities of their day, it's rather common for probing questions to surface. These sometimes include even spiritual questions, such as, How good do you have to be to enter heaven? What do I really believe about God? If you have found yourself asking these questions, we hope you will find these thoughts helpful in your search for answers.

1. *How good do you have to be to get into heaven?*

I (Dillon) recently read about a survey that reported that a

majority of people still believe there is a hell, but less than one percent of those people believe they will go there. Most people think
they are just as good as anyone else—maybe even better. But what if
the average "good person" doesn't make it?

So how good *does* a person have to be to get into heaven? The
short answer, according to Jesus, is that you must be perfect or you
won't get in. In Matthew's Gospel, Jesus told His listeners, "I tell you
that unless your righteousness surpasses that of the Pharisees and
the teachers of the law, *you will certainly not enter the kingdom of
heaven*"[284] (emphasis added). At that time the Pharisees tried to keep
over 500 laws every day to please God. Although the religious leaders
didn't always accomplish their goal, the average person thought he
or she could live as righteously as the teachers of the law. That's why
everyone was shocked when Jesus said you have to go *beyond* the
level of the Pharisees to make it.

A little later, Jesus clarified this even further. He said, "Be perfect,
therefore, as your heavenly Father is perfect."[285] In other words, if
you're not as perfect as God, don't even *think* you'll make it into
heaven.

How does this apply to us? Do you think God will let *you* into
heaven? Since we could never be good enough to stand before God,
Jesus provides His righteousness to us as a free gift. He said, "God
sent not his Son into the world to condemn the world, but to save the
world through him."[286] Peter writes, "Christ died for your sins once
for all, the righteous for the unrighteous, to bring you to God."[287]

2. *Would you like Jesus to connect you with God?*

The apostle Paul says, "God made him [Jesus] who knew no sin
to be sin for us, so that in him we might become the righteousness
of God."[288] This means that when Jesus was crucified on the cross,
God picked up our sins along with the sins of the entire world and
placed them upon Jesus. Jesus became guilty of all of our sins in a
legal sense. Paul was quick to point out that Jesus had no sins of His
own, but that He became our substitute. Jesus died so we could have
eternal life (Romans 6:23; John 11:25-26).

Paul writes that God is offering this new life through Christ as a free gift when you place your faith in Him. "This righteousness from God comes through *faith* in Jesus Christ to all who believe. There is no difference…[they] are justified freely *by His grace*"[289] (emphasis added). So whether you have struggled with extremely difficult life choices or consider yourself just an everyday person who has made simple mistakes, God is willing to provide the perfect righteousness you need to stand before Him.

I (John) taped a television program with a young man who had placed his trust in Christ after living his life as a homosexual prostitute. A month after taping that program, this man died from AIDS. My friend Dr. Erwin Lutzer also knew this man. One day when we were taping a broadcast together, Dr. Lutzer referred to this person, saying, "Think of two books. The first is called *The Life and Times of Roger* (not his real name). A second book is called *The Life and Times of Jesus Christ*. When you open the covers of *The Life and Times of Roger,* you see all the sins of Roger's life. There, for everyone to witness, are lust and broken relationships. Roger had over 1,100 sexual partners during his life, leaving a trail of lies, anger, and hurt toward many of those around him. Yet if you open the cover of the second book, *The Life and Times of Jesus Christ,* these pages contain all of His life's perfections and absolute purity.

"Now picture what happens the moment Roger placed his faith in Christ. God rips the covers off both books. He then places the contents of *The Life and Times of Jesus Christ* inside the covers of Roger's book. After that, every time God opens *The Life and Times of Roger,* he sees only the perfect life of Christ. This is what justification by faith truly means."

3. How much faith do I need to get into heaven?

The Bible says, "Believe in the Lord Jesus and you will be saved."[290] Believing on Jesus is not just accepting facts about Jesus, though these facts are the foundation for faith. Just believing that Christ lived, died on the cross, and rose from the dead is not true faith. True faith is when you transfer all of your *trust* to Jesus.

One day a famous tightrope walker strung a wire across Niagara Falls. In front of a crowd of people, he jumped up on the wire and walked from the Canadian side to the American side and back again. Many people gathered to watch him. Then he put a wheelbarrow on the wire and filled it with sandbags weighing over 200 pounds. He successfully took that wheelbarrow with the sandbags across the falls and back. Then, he paused and asked the people who were gathered, "How many of you think I could place a *person* in this wheelbarrow and take him across the falls? Raise your hand." They all raised their hands, saying, "We believe you can do it." He then asked, "Who will be the first to get in?" No one would trust him with *their* life.

Jesus asks us, "Do you believe I am the Son of God who died for your sins, the one who can forgive you and offer you eternal life?"

You respond, "Lord, I believe."

Then Jesus says, "Then get into My wheelbarrow. Entrust your eternal destiny into My hands alone." If you will, Jesus promises that He will save you, enter your life, and enable you to live with power over sin. He will also give you eternal life. If you have not entrusted yourself into Jesus' hands, placing your faith solely in Him, why not now? The Bible promises, "Everyone who calls on the name of the Lord will be saved."[291] That "everyone" includes *you* the moment you place your faith in Christ alone.

4. How much faith do you need?

Beginning a relationship with Christ doesn't require a lot of faith. What is important is that you have faith, and that your faith has the proper focus.

Imagine that you're standing in an apartment building, two stories up. All of the exits are closed, you cannot leave the building, and a fire has just started. Firemen arrive, carrying a rescue net. One of the firefighters looks up at you and shouts, "Jump!"

You look down and shout back, "No way!"

The fireman replies, "What choice do you have? If you stay there, you'll die."

"But I don't have enough faith."

"You don't have to have a *lot* of faith. Just step off of the building. We'll catch you."

In terms of Christ saving us, He doesn't require a lot of faith—just enough to step out and place ourselves in His hands. It's Jesus who does the saving, just like it's the firemen who help people in need of rescue. Whether your faith is big or small is not the issue; it is Jesus who does the saving.

But what if after you had jumped, you discovered the firemen were not holding a net? Would you still be rescued? No! You would be in a desperate situation because you had put your faith in the wrong object. True faith must include stepping out into the unknown, but it also involves faith in a known reality, Jesus Christ.

5. *How do I begin a relationship with God?*

God knows our hearts and is not as concerned with our words as He is with our attitude. The following is just a suggested prayer. You can pray your own prayer. It's not the specific prayer that saves you; it is trusting in Christ that saves you.

> *Dear Lord Jesus, I admit that I have sinned. I know I cannot save myself. Thank You for dying on the cross. I believe that Your death was for me, and I receive Your sacrifice on my behalf. I now transfer all of my trust from myself to You. I open the door of my life to You and by faith receive You as my Savior and Lord. Thank You for forgiving my sins and giving me eternal life. Amen.*

6. *How do you know that Christ is in your life?*

"Here I am! I stand at the door and knock. If anyone hears my voice and opens the door, I will come in."[292] Christ said that if anyone will invite Him into their life, He will enter their life.

The apostle John wrote, "I write these things to you who believe in the name of the Son of God so that you may know that you have eternal life."[293] If you have entrusted yourself to Christ and have believed in Him, the Scripture says God wants you to *know*—not guess—that you have eternal life.

In Romans 10:13, the apostle Paul said that "Everyone who calls on the name of the Lord will be saved." He promises to save when you call and trust in Christ. "To all who received him, to those who believed in his name, he gave the right to become children of God."[294]

7. Now what?

Begin by sharing about your decision with someone you know. Tell him or her about the change that has taken place in your life. Then follow through on your decision by learning more about Jesus Christ. This includes reading God's Word, going to a Bible-teaching church, spending time with other followers of Christ, and beginning to serve others from the overflow of your transformed life.

Finally, please let us know about your choice to follow Jesus. We would love to know about your spiritual commitment. Please contact us with your story at staff@johnankerberg.org or write us at:[295]

The Ankerberg Theological Research Institute
P.O. Box 8977
Chattanooga, TN 37414 USA

Seven Ways to Make a Positive Difference in the Middle East

1. Pray for Those Involved

The apostle Paul taught his protégé Timothy the all-inclusive nature of prayer when he wrote, "I urge you, first of all, to pray for all people. As you make your requests, plead for God's mercy upon them, and give thanks. Pray this way for kings and all others who are in authority, so that we can live in peace and quietness, in godliness and dignity. This is good and pleases God our Savior, for he wants everyone to be saved and to understand the truth."[296] Our prayers should include prayers for our government and its leaders, for Israel's peace, the physical health of soldiers and civilians on all sides, Christian brothers and sisters of every culture and country, and the spiritual condition of each person's life, as well as for God's will to be done.

While the Bible is clear that Israel has a special, eternal relationship with God as a nation, this does not negate the need to pray even for those who speak against and attack this nation. Some Christian leaders, in their zeal to show support for Israel, speak blatantly against any negotiations regarding land or even lives with other groups. Though positively motivated, this attitude stands in contrast to biblical teaching that promotes love as the highest value (1 Corinthians 13:13), and especially neglects Christians, churches, and ministry organizations serving in areas of conflict.

2. Create Awareness

A major goal of *Middle East Meltdown* is to promote a healthy awareness of what is really taking place in the Middle East. For instance, it helps the public greatly to know that the recently strengthened stands on U.S. border patrol and immigration stem not only from illegal immigration, but also from the very real concern of terrorist activities along America's borders. The politics in our media headlines often promote the issue as a racially charged offense toward Mexican immigration. While this may sometimes be the case, it is not the complete picture.

It is also important to increase awareness of these issues because of the spiritual implications. For example, if biblical prophecy *does* speak about the current Middle East issues in an accurate way, then this should encourage deepened study and reflection of the Jewish and Christian Scriptures. In doing so, God's Word is promoted (a positive desire in Christianity) and lives can be transformed in many ways even outside of the Middle Eastern issues discussed.

Hebrews 4:12 says, "The word of God is living and active. Sharper than any double-edged sword, it penetrates even to dividing soul and spirit, joints and marrow; it judges the thoughts and attitudes of the heart." Simply helping point friends, family, co-workers, and others toward Scripture for answers on today's significant issues helps provide insights on those issues. It also provides an opportunity for God's living Word to perform its life-changing work.

3. Support Those in Need

By support, we mean to give something besides or in addition to money. Several organizations exist, both Christian and non-Christian, that are currently serving the most afflicted Middle Eastern areas. Provisions of basic necessities such as food, clean water, housing, blankets, clothing, job training, home construction resources, Bibles and literacy materials, the building of schools, orphanages, assistance to widows, and help for displaced and separated families all offer both tremendous challenges and opportunities.

Some good organizations include:

- Campus Crusade for Christ/Bibles for the Middle East: https://give2.ccci.org/featured/middleeast-cw

- Frontiers: www.frontiers.org

- The Red Cross: www.RedCross.org

- Samaritan's Purse: www.samaritanspurse.org
- World Relief: www.wr.org
- World Vision: www.worldvision.org

Please see www.usaid.gov for a more comprehensive listing of humanitarian needs and www.interaction.org/mideast for supporting organizations.

4. Give Financially

There are certainly financial needs as well. One recent analysis of just the Israeli-Hezbollah conflict of August 2006 showed the staggering costs of war, as indicated in the chart below.

Several organizations exist that are committed to humanitarian aid in these countries. Most of the organizations listed in the previous section can also help you offer financial assistance.

COST OF WAR FOR ISRAEL
(data from the Israeli embassy in Washington)

Israeli Casualties:
- 159 dead: 116 soldiers, 43 civilians
- 2,015 people injured, 1,318 of them victims of shock

Israeli Citizens Affected:
- 500,000 displaced
- 7,600 damages claims have been filed [up to time of this writing]

Economic Damage:
- Cost of war: approximately $11.3 billion
- Estimated 1.5 percent loss of gross domestic product
- Estimated $460 million in aid will be transferred to local governments and emergency services in the north
- Tourism down approximately 20 percent
- Hotels in northern Israel have lost approximately $27 million
- Total expected damage to tourism industry: approximately $222 million
- Manufacturers in northern Israel lost approximately $67 to $89 million

COST OF WAR FOR LEBANON
(data from the U.N. Office for the Coordination of Humanitarian Affairs)

1,152 Lebanese have been killed and some 3,700 wounded.

An estimated 200,000 Lebanese have returned to their home areas... according to the HRC, leaving the estimated number of internally displaced persons (IDPs) in Lebanon currently at just over 700,000.

The HRC also reports that more than 40 percent of people previously sheltering in schools and other public centers have left for their home areas.

An estimated 60,000 Lebanese are believed to have spontaneously returned from Syria...according to the Office of the United Nations High Commissioner for Refugees (UNHCR).

However, the HRC estimates that some 15,000 housing units have been destroyed in Lebanon.

An initial assessment by the United Nations Interim Force in Lebanon (UNIFIL) indicates extensive damage to civilian housing in southern Lebanon: in the village of Tayyabah, 80 percent of homes have been destroyed; 50 percent in Markaba and Qantarah, and 30 percent in Mays al Jabal.

Media reports suggest bombing damage in Lebanon tops $2.6 billion, though this number is likely to rise as more detailed assessments are done.[297]

5. Submit to Governing Authorities

In Romans 13:1-2 the apostle Paul tells Christians, "Everyone must submit himself to the governing authorities, for there is no authority except that which God has established. The authorities that exist have been established by God. Consequently, he who rebels against the authority is rebelling against what God has instituted, and those who do so will bring judgment on themselves." A contemporary way of wording this teaching would be to say, "Everyone obey the law, because God put it there. When you rebel against the government, you're asking for trouble!" God's Word is very clear that an anarchist attitude is unacceptable for a follower of Christ.

Unfortunately, in the current War on Terror, one of the great weaknesses of America has been its divided public. When people speak poorly of our military and government regarding the war in Iraq and don't show support for our troops, it provides greater motivation to those attempting to bring destruction to America's freedom. As Christians, our goal should be to submit to our government's leadership, regardless of our personal opinions, unless a government refuses to allow religious freedom to worship Jesus Christ.[298]

6. If Possible, Go to Those in Need

While not always possible, there are many opportunities for individuals and groups to physically go to those in need of assistance. One *Time* magazine article reports:

> As the war in Iraq moves into its next phase, Christian missionaries are moving forward with their own battle plans: to distribute humanitarian aid and spread the gospel to the region's Muslims.[299]

Southern Baptist Theological Seminary president Dr. Albert Mohler well stated the case by noting:

> It would be an appalling tragedy if America were to lead this coalition and send young American men and women into battle, to expend such military effort, to then leave in place a regime that would lack respect for religious liberty. I think one of the major Christian concerns, and one of my personal concerns, is to see religious liberty, religious freedom, take a prominent position in the vision of freedom that America holds up to the world.[300]

Mission organizations such as Frontiers (www.frontiers.org) and Campus Crusade for Christ (www.ccci.org) have invested considerable effort toward providing opportunities for those who desire to serve in the Middle Eastern and Arab nations. In addition, several government groups currently serve in the Lebanon-Israeli border area providing humanitarian relief. An updated list of these opportunities can be found at www.alertnet.org.[301]

7. Live a Life of Integrity

Ultimately, the best way to make a difference is to live a life of integrity. Best-selling author Dr. Charles Swindoll wrote,

> The longer I live, the more I realize the impact of attitude on life. Attitude, to me, is more important than facts. It is more important than the past, the education, the money, than circumstances, than failure, than successes, than what other people think or say or do. It is more important than appearance, giftedness or skill. It will make or break a company...a church...a home. The remarkable thing is we have a choice every day regarding the attitude we will embrace for that day. We cannot change our past...we cannot change the fact that people will act in a certain way. We cannot change the inevitable. The only thing we can do is play on the one string we have, and that is our attitude. I am convinced that life is 10% what happens to me and 90% of how I react to it. And so it is with you...we are in charge of our attitudes.[302]

We impact others around us most when our beliefs and actions are consistent. Jesus Himself set the example by coming to earth to live a life of integrity in the midst of people in need. He, "who, being in very nature God, did not consider equality with God something to be grasped, but made himself nothing, taking the very nature of a servant, being made in human likeness. And being found in appearance as a man, he humbled himself and became obedient to death—even death on a cross!"[303]

The greatest way to make an impact in the Middle East? Start by living a life that reflects personal integrity and models Jesus Christ.

Appendix B:

The Nations of Ezekiel 38–39

There has been much discussion in this book regarding the nations of Ezekiel 38–39. While we did not include a detailed study of these chapters, we have provided a quick-reference chart listing the original nations and their modern equivalents. A special thanks goes to the works of Dr. John Walvoord and Dr. Mark Hitchcock for the research used in compiling this chart.

> When the battle of Gog and Magog begins, Israel will be in her land in peace and safety (Ezek. 38:8,11,14). Six countries will then attack Israel. Five of them are mentioned by name (Persia, Cush, Put, Gomer, and Beth Togarmah; 38:5-6), and the sixth, "the land of Magog," undoubtedly relates to a portion of the former Soviet Union, for it will go against Israel from "the far north" (38:15; 39:2). Perhaps only some of the states of the former Soviet Union will participate in this war.[304]

Original name	Current name
Rosh	Russia, though possibly only a portion of it. During Ezekiel's time, the people of Rosh included people living north of the Black Sea.
Magog	The areas of Kazakhstan, Kirghizia, Uzbekistan, Turkmenistan, Tajikistan, and possibly including Afghanistan
Meshech	Portions of Turkey
Tubal	Portions of Turkey
Persia	Iran
Cush/Ethiopia	Sudan (different from modern Ethiopia)
Put	Possibly Libya (Put was historically the land west of Egypt)

Gomer	Portions of Turkey
Beth-togarmah	Portions of Turkey

Note: Egypt, Pakistan, and Iraq are not listed in this prophecy, though they are major Islamic nations. Some argue that Pakistan may be included as one of the nations above, such as in connection with Persia (Iran). Egypt is listed in several other prophecies, though some suggest its current peace treaty keeps it from being listed in Ezekiel 38–39. Iraq may well be left out due to its predominance in the Tribulation period as the world capital in Babylon—that is, if the Babylon in Revelation refers to the ancient city located in modern Iraq.[305]

For a visual depiction of how these nations appear on a map, see the Web site http://lastday.info/map.html.

Important Dates in Israel's Recent History

1948   The creation of the state of Israel and the War of Independence. Jerusalem is divided, with east Jerusalem under Jordanian rule. The Arab legion captures the old city and destroys the Jewish quarter, including 58 Jewish religious sites. The population at that time is 99,320 Jews, 36,680 Muslims, and 31,300 Christians.

1949   Jordan defies Armistice Treaty, which assured free access to the Western Wall.

1951   King Abdullah of Jordan is assassinated by Muslim Arabs atop the Temple Mount.

1967   The Six-Day War—Jerusalem is reunited under Jewish sovereignty. Knesset passes law for the protection of holy places of all faiths.

1973   Yom Kippur (Day of Atonement) War, October 6, 1973—the holiest day of the year for the Jews.

Egypt attacked Israel across the Sinai, and Syria invaded the Golan Heights. Israel lost 500 tanks and 49 aircraft (including 14 F-4 Phantoms) in the first three days of battle.

On the Golan Heights, Syria, with 1,400 tanks, rolled through Israeli defenses and moved to the edge of Galilee.

Israeli military leader Moshe Dayan's assessment: "The situation is desperate. Everything is lost. We must withdraw." He instigated the readiness of the Samson Option if it was needed.

1979   Egypt and Israel sign peace treaty.

1993   On September 13, Israel and the Palestine Liberation Organization (PLO) sign the Oslo Accords.

1995   Israel and Jordan sign peace treaty.

2006   Israel and Hezbollah battle in southern Lebanon in August. Nearly 1,200 people in Lebanon and 157 people in Israel are killed. Iran continues plans for nuclear development, posing as a future threat against its enemies, including Israel.

Notes

1. Susan Tolchin, "Mixed Feelings, Happy Trade-Offs," in *Earth Times,* August 2, 1993.

2. Transcripts of the August 26, 2006 edition of *The Early Show* on CBS.

3. "Homegrown Terrorists a Very Big Threat," *CNN News,* June 23, 2006. Accessed at http://www.cnn.com/2006/US/06/23/kent.cnna/index.html.

4. For examples of how serious this movement is, see http://www.templeinstitute.org/main.htm and http://www.templemountfaithful.org.

5. Joel Rosenberg, "Canadian Terror Plot Headlines Ripped from *The Last Days,*" at http://www.leftbehind.com/channelfree.asp?pageid=1300&channelID=175.

6. Transcript obtained from http://www.foxnews.com/story/0,2933,211527,00.html. August 30,2006.

7. For the full text of this resolution, please see http://www.un.org/News/Press/docs//2006/sc8792.doc.htm.

8. George W. Bush, The National Security Strategy of the United States of America, March 2006. Accessed at http://www.whitehouse.gov/nsc/nss/2006/nss2006.pdf.

9. As released in the 2006 study "Five Years Later: 9/11 Attacks Show No Lasting Influence on Americans' Faith" by the Barna Group. Accessed at http://www.barna.org/FlexPage.aspx?Page=BarnaUpdate&BarnaUpdateID=244.

10. "Nuclear 9/11: Will It Happen?" Bulletin of the Atomic Scientists, September/October 2006, pp. 26-27.

11. John Mueller, "Is There Still a Terrorist Threat?" *Foreign Affairs,* September/October 2006, p. 2.

12. The *9/11 Digital Archive* shares stories reflective of many others at www.911digitalarchive.org.

13. Weston Kosova and David Gerlach, "Terror in Our Time," *Newsweek,* August 28, 2006, pp. 54-55.

14. Please note: Quoted transcripts of *The John Ankerberg Show* have been edited for space and clarity. Full transcripts for most interviews can be purchased at www.johnankerberg.org.

15. For more on this organization, see http://www.templemountfaithful.org.

16. Thomas Ice and Randall Price, *Ready to Rebuild* (Eugene, OR: Harvest House, 1992), p. 139.

17. "Disturbance Diverts London-D.C. Flight," Associated Press, August 16, 2006. Accessed at http://www.breitbart.com/news/2006/08/16/ D8JHJGMO0.html.

18. March 2006 interview for *The John Ankerburg Show*. Available as program three of the series "Where Is Islam Taking the World?" at www.johnankerberg.org.

19. Including the dark history of Christianity. Though beyond the scope of this book, the Caner brothers effectively discuss the Crusades at length in *Christian Jihad* (Grand Rapids, MI: Kregel, 2004).

20. "All About Islam." Accessed at http://www.simpletoremember.com/vitals/ Islam.Judaism.htm.

21. Dr. Anis Shorrosh, from "Eight Well-Known Evangelical Christian Scholars from Different Disciplines Advise Christians on Issues Facing Them Today," transcript from The Ankerberg Theological Research Institute available at www.johnankerberg.org.

22. Adapted from Norman L. Geisler and Abdul Saleeb, *Answering Islam* (Grand Rapids, MI: Baker Books, 1993), pp. 293-94.

23. Emir Fethi Caner and Ergun Mehmet Caner, *More Than a Prophet: An Insider's Response to Muslim Beliefs About Jesus & Christianity* (Grand Rapids, MI: Kregel, 2003), p. 71.

24. Ibid., p. 7.

25. Ibid., pp. 126-27.

26. Statement of Osama bin Laden, Hindukush Mountains, Khurasan, Afghanistan, Friday September 4, 1996.

27. Cited in Hal Lindsey, *The Final Battle* (Palos Verdes, CA: Western Front, Ltd., 1995).

28. As cited at http://www.csmonitor.com/2006/0510/p01s04-wome.html.

29. As cited at http://www.iht.com/articles/2005/12/11/news/letter.php.

30. Ibid.

31. Ibid.

32. Ibid.

33. As cited at http://www.globalsecurity.org/military/ops/iran-strikes-2006. htm.

34. Abdullah Al-Araby, *The Islamization of America* (Los Angeles, CA: The Pen vs. The Sword, 2003), p. 19.

35. Robert Spencer, *The Politically Incorrect Guide to Islam* (Washington, D.C.: Regnery Publishing, 2005), p. 209.

36. John Ankerberg and John Weldon, *The Facts on Islam* (Eugene, OR: Harvest House, 1998), p. 13.

37. Amy Waldman, "Prophetic Justice," *The Atlantic Monthly,* October 2006, p. 87.

38. Robert Spencer, *Islam Unveiled* (San Francisco, CA: Encounter Books, 2002), p. 167.

39. Victor Mordecai, *Is Fanatic Islam a Global Threat?* (Jerusalem: Victor Mordecai, 1997), p. 24.

40. Michael R. Licona, *Paul Meets Muhammad: A Christian-Muslim Debate on the Resurrection* (Grand Rapids, MI: Baker Books, 2006), p. 13.

41. Roy Oksnevad and Dotsey Welliver, *The Gospel for Islam: Reaching Muslims in North America* (Wheaton, IL: EMIS, 2001), pp. v-vi.

42. The complete report can be accessed online at http://freedomhouse.org/religion. A special thanks to the research staff at the Freedom House for their efforts on this project.

43. "Saudi Publications on Hate Ideology Fill American Mosques," Center for Religious Freedom, January 28, 2005. Accessed at http://www.freedomhouse.org/religion/news/bn2005/bn-2005-01-28.htm.

44. "Pakistani Clerics, Scholars Want Pope Removed," CNN, September 21, 2006. Accessed at http://www.cnn.com/2006/WORLD/asiapcf/09/21/pakistan.pope.ap/index.html.

45. "U.S. Should Press Pakistan to Repeal Blasphemy Law," Center for Religious Freedom, July 13, 2005. Accessed at http://www.freedomhouse.org/religion/news/bn2005/bn-2005-07-14.htm.

46. John Ankerberg and John Weldon, *Fast Facts on Islam* (Eugene, OR: Harvest House, 2001), p. 22.

47. From the http://www.memri.org archives. Cited at Joel Rosenberg, "Invade Gaza, Take Down Hamastan," July 5, 2006. Accessed at http://joelrosenberg.blogspot.com/2006_07_01_joelrosenberg_archive.html.

48. Paul Marshall, "To Engage Moderate Muslims, We Must Understand Radical Islam," Religion News Service, May 23, 2005. Accessed at http://www.freedomhouse.org/religion/news/bn2005/bn-2005-05-23.htm.

49. "Syria," *Religious Freedom World Report*. Accessed at http://www.religious-freedom.com/.

50. "Saudi Arabia," *Religious Freedom World Report*. Accessed at http://www.religiousfreedom.com/.

51. Ibid.

52. "Muslim Britain: More People Attend Mosques than Church of England," January 27, 2004. Accessed at http://jihadwatch.org/dhimmiwatch/archives/000743.php.

53. Patrick Hennessy and Melissa Kite, "Poll reveals 40pc of Muslims want sharia law in UK," *Telegraph*, February 19, 2006. Accessed at http://www.telegraph.co.uk/news/main.jhtml?xml=/news/2006/02/19/nsharia19.xml.

54. Rusty Wright, "Why Radical Muslims Hate You," *The Plain Truth*, September/October 2004, pp. 6-9. Accessed online at http://www.probe.org/content/view/835/65/.

55. Matthew 5:44 NASB.

56. Romans 13:4.

57. Rusty Wright, "Why Radical Muslims Hate You," *The Plain Truth*, September/October 2004, pp. 6-9. Accessed online at http://www.probe.org/content/view/835/65/.

58. 1 Chronicles 12:32; Esther 1:13.

59. Acts 17:16-34. Paul also served as part of a multicultural leadership team, a setup that allowed for a greater understanding of diversity. See Acts 13:1-3.

60. During an interview on *The John Ankerberg Show*, "The Middle East, War on Terrorism, and the Hope for Peace," 2002.

61. Frederick Kenyon, *The Bible and Archaeology* (New York: Harper & Row, 1940), pp. 288-89.

62. For more on this book from a Christian perspective, see Michael Easley, John Ankerberg, and Dillon Burroughs, *The Da Vinci Code Controversy* (Chicago, IL: Moody, 2006).

63. For a conservative Christian response to this book, see Dillon Burroughs, *Misquotes in* Misquoting Jesus (Ann Arbor, MI: Nimble Books, 2006).

64. For more information on this book from a Christian perspective, order

the video or transcripts for "From Skepticism to Belief" at www.johnan-kerberg.org.

65. For more on the Gospel of Judas, see Patrick Zukeran, "A Brief Overview of the Gospel of Judas," 2006. Accessed at http://www.probe.org/content/view/1370/64/.

66. Shibley Telhami, "The Persian Gulf: Understanding the American Oil Strategy," *The Brookings Review,* Spring 2002, pp. 32-35. Accessed at http://www.brookings.edu/press/REVIEW/spring2002/telhami.htm.

67. Richard Heinburg, unofficial leader of the Peak Oil movement, as cited by Bryan Urstadt, "Imagine There's No Oil," *Harper's Magazine,* August 2006, p. 31.

68. Brendan Murray, "Bush Leverage with Russia, Iran, China Falls as Oil Prices Rise," May 1, 2006. Accessed at http://www.bloomberg.com/apps/news?pid=10000087&sid=ar4D7HVGikXo&refer=top_world_news.

69. "Trade Deficit Surges to Record $68 Billion in July on Rising Oil Prices," AP News, September 12, 2006. Accessed at http://www.foxnews.com/story/0,2933,213447,00.html.

70. Stephen Leeb, *The Coming Economic Crisis* (New York: Warner Business, 2006), p. 25.

71. Drake Bennett, *The Boston Globe,* February 26, 2006. Accessed at http://www.boston.com/news/globe/ideas/articles/2006/02/26/oil_futures/?page=full.

72. Peter Tertzakian, in *Iran the Coming Crisis: Radical Islam, Oil, and the Nuclear Threat* (Sisters, OR: Multnomah, 2006), p. 97.

73. Ibid., p. 98.

74. James Inhofe, "Seven Reasons Why Israel Is Entitled to the Land," March 4, 2002. Transcript accessed at http://christianactionforisrael.org/inhofe.html.

75. Kari Huss, "In China's Oil Quest, No Deal Is Too Unsavory," MSNBC News, May 4, 2006. Accessed http://www.msnbc.msn.com/id/12501039/.

76. From http://www.prophecynewswatch.com/.

77. "Iran Says Sanctions Over Nuclear Row Unlikely," *Reuters,* April 24, 2006. Accessed at http://msnbc.msn.com/id/12465457/.

78. Roger Howard, "Oil Price Warfare," *The National Interest,* September/October 2006, p. 85.

79. Mortimer B. Zuckerman, "Getting Serious About Oil," *U.S. News & World Report,* August 7, 2006. Accessed online at http://www.usnews.com/usnews/opinion/articles/060730/7edit.htm.

80. From the Energy Information Administration at http://www.eia.doe.gov/emeu/cabs/topworldtables1_2.html.

81. Totals from http://www.infoplease.com/ipa/A0872964.html.

82. Mark Hitchcock, *Iran: The Coming Crisis* (Sisters, OR: Multnomah, 2006), p. 103.

83. "Iran: Atomic Project Is Peaceful," CNN, August 26, 2006. Accessed at http://www.cnn.com/2006/WORLD/meast/08/26/iran.nuclear/index.html.

84. Accessed at http://www.foxnews.com/story/0,2933,209610,00.html.

85. Mark Hitchcock, *Iran: The Coming Crisis* (Sisters, OR: Multnomah, 2006), p. 103.

86. Cited in Randall Price, *Unholy War: America, Israel and Radical Islam* (Eugene, OR: Harvest House, 2001), p. 17.

87. During an interview on *The John Ankerberg Show,* 1991.

88. Mohammed Tawfeeq, "Al Qaeda in Iraq Followers Told to Kill 'At Least One American,'" September 7, 2006. Accessed at http://www.cnn.com/2006/WORLD/meast/09/07/iraq.main/index.html.

89. Joel Rosenberg, "Ahmadinejad Coming to U.S. to Challenge Bush for Global Supremacy," September 6, 2006. Accessed at http://joelrosenberg.blogspot.com.

90. "Iranian envoy calls for Russia's more active role in Middle East," *Islamic Republic News Agency,* July 25, 2006. Accessed at http://www.irna.ir/en/news/view/menu-236/0607262850103624.htm.

91. Ibid.

92. "Russian Troops Make First Mideast Foray in Lebanon for Centuries," AFP News, September 27, 2006. Accessed at http://www.spacewar.com/reports/Russian_Troops_Make_First_Mideast_Foray_In_Lebanon_For_Centuries_999.html.

93. Special thanks on this section to Kenneth R. Timmerman, "Iranian President

Sees End of World Order," January 24, 2006. Accessed at http://www. newsmax.com/archives/articles/2006/1/23/173442.shtml?s=lh.

94. Ibid.

95. English transcript accessed at http://www.npr.org/templates/story/story. php?storyId=6105334. Emphases added.

96. Charles Krauthammer, "In Iran, Arming for Armageddon," *Washington Post*, Friday, December 16, 2005; p. A35. Accessed online at http://www.washingtonpost.com/wp-dyn/content/article/2005/12/15/AR2005121501428. html.

97. Joel Rosenberg, *Flash Traffic Update* email subscription, September 7, 2006.

98. Peter L. Bergen, *The Osama bin Laden I Know* (New York: Free Press, 2006), p. 169.

99. Lawrence Wright, *The Looming Tower: Al-Qaeda and the Road to 9/11* (New York: Alfred A. Knopf, 2006), p. 371.

100. Quoted from an October 2006 support letter from The Ankerberg Theological Research Institute.

101. Martin and Susan J. Tolchin, *A World United* (Lanham: Rowman & Littlefield, 2006), p. 43.

102. *Paula Zahn Now*, July 31, 2006. Transcripts accessed at http://transcripts. cnn.com/TRANSCRIPTS/0607/31/pzn.01.html.

103. As noted at http://www.usaid.gov/iran/.

104. Including a portion of the proceeds from this book.

105. Tony Blankley, *The West's Last Chance* (Washington, D.C.: Regnery, 2006), p. 129.

106. Ibid., pp. 129-30.

107. From a study released on Harris Interactive at http://www.harrisinteractive.com/harris_poll/index.asp?PID=437.

108. Ron Suskind, *The One Percent Doctrine* (New York: Simon & Schuster, 2006), p. 329.

109. From a May 12, 2006 Harris Interactive poll at http://www.harrisinteractive.com/harris_poll/index.asp?PID=664.

110. Heather May and Christopher Smart, "Salt Lake sounds off in protest and support," *The Salt Lake Tribune*, August 31, 2006.

111. Thomas E. Ricks, *Fiasco: The American Military Adventure in Iraq* (New

York: The Penguin Press, 2006), p. 4. A similar case, also implicating religious groups, is presented very negatively by the popular book by Kevin
Phillips, *American Theocracy* (New York: Viking Adult, 2006).

112. Andrew Taylor, "Senate Votes to Restore Bin Laden Unit," AP Report,
September 7, 2006. Accessed at http://www.guardian.co.uk/worldlatest/
story/0,,-6065501,00.html.

113. "Bush insights it's 'just a matter of time' until bin Laden caught," *The
Houston Chronicle,* September 6, 2006. Accessed at http://www.chron.
com/disp/story.mpl/nation/4168667.html.

114. Mentioned during a CNN interview with George W. Bush transcribed at
http://www.cnn.com/2006/POLITICS/09/20/bush.intv/index.html.

115. "Bin Laden Expert Steps Forward," from the CBS program *60 Minutes.*
Accessed   at   http://www.cbsnews.com/stories/2004/11/12/60minutes/
main655407.shtml.

116. The complete September 21, 2006 statement can be found at http://www.
foxnews.com/story/0,2933,215042,00.html.

117. Romans 13:1-2,5.

118. President George W. Bush, War on Terror speech, September 6, 2006.
Transcript accessed at http://www.cnn.com/2006/POLITICS/09/06/bush.
transcript/index.html.

119. "Pilgrims Progress," *Newsweek,* August 14, 2006.

120. John Hagee, *Jerusalem Countdown* (Lake Mary, FL: Frontline, 2006), p.1.

121. John Wheeler, Jr., *Christian American* 5:2 (February 1994), as cited in Randall Price, *Jerusalem in Prophecy* (Eugene, OR: Harvest House, 1998), p.
146.

122. "Netanyahu defends Jerusalem housing project," March 18, 1997. Accessed
at http://www.cnn.com/WORLD/9703/18/israel/index.html.

123. For those interested, there is additional material on this topic at http://
www.templemount.org/tempprep.html.

124. "Current Events in Light of Biblical Prophecy" transcript, program 3.
Available for purchase at www.johnankerberg.org.

125. Seymour M. Hersh, *The Samson Option* (New York: Random House,
1991).

126. Judges 13–16.

127. "[Egyptian president] Sadat further quoted Kissinger as saying. 'It was
serious, more serious than you can imagine.' Israel had at least three

warheads and was preparing to use them, Sadat told Heikal." Hersh, *The Samson Option* (New York: Random House, 1991), p. 231.

128. Accessed at http://joelrosenberg.blogspot.com/2006_08_01_joelrosenberg_archive.html.

129. Daniel Pipes, "If I Forget Thee: Does Jerusalem Really Matter to Islam?" *New Republic*, April 28, 1997. Accessed at http://www.danielpipes.org/article/281.

130. "Let's Face It: Israel's Refugees (in Hebrew)," *Walla News*, August 10, 2006. Accessed at http://finance.walla.co.il/?w=/3402/955907.

131. Stephen Farrel, "The Times Interview with Ehud Olmert: full transcript," *Times Online*, August 2, 2006. Accessed at http://www.timesonline.co.uk/article/0,,251-2296832,00.html.

132. "Hezbollah," Council on Foreign Relations, July 17, 2006. Accessed at http://www.cfr.org/publication/9155.

133. Ibid., note the corresponding links at this source for additional resources.

134. *The Jerusalem Quarterly*, no. Forty-Eight, Fall 1988. Accessed at http://www.ict.org.il/Articles/Hiz_letter.htm. This is a slightly abridged translation of "Nass al-Risala al-Maftuha allati wajahaha Hizballah ila-l -Mustad'afin fi Lubnan wa-l -Alam," published February 16, 1985 in *al-Safir* (Beirut), and also in a separate brochure. It carries the unmistakable imprint of Sheikh Muhammad Hussein Fadlallah, the Hezbollah mentor, and is inspired by his book *Ma'maal-Quwma fi-l -Islam* (Beirut, 1979). See also his article in *al-Muntalak* (Beirut), October 1986.

135. Ibid.

136. See http://www.jewishvirtuallibrary.org/jsource/myths/mf10.html for an excellent discussion of these boundaries in modern times.

137. "The Al-Qaida-Hizballah Connection," Institute for Counter-Terrorism at the Interdisciplinary Center Herzliya, February 26, 2002. Accessed at http://www.ict.org.il/articles/articledet.cfm?articleid=425.

138. Christopher Dickery and Babak Dehghanpisheh, "Torn to Shreds," *Newsweek*, July 31, 2006, p. 24.

139. "Hezbollah," at http://en.wikipedia.org/wiki/Hezbollah.

140. "U.S. Rejects Syrian Call for Ceasefire," CBC News, July 23, 2006. Accessed at http://www.cbc.ca/story/world/national/2006/07/23/syria-lebanon.html.

141. "Annan: Syria Promises to Impose Arms Embargo on Hezbollah,"

CNN News, September 1, 2006. Accessed at http://www.cnn.com/2006/ WORLD/meast/09/01/mideast.annan.assad/index.html.

142. "Syria Opposes U.N. Force on Border," *CNN News,* August 24, 2006. Accessed at http://www.cnn.com/2006/WORLD/meast/08/24/mideast. main/index.html.

143. Gary H. Kah, "War with Iraq: The Aftermath," http://www.johnankerberg. org/Articles/editors-choice/ECo403W4.htm.

144. Borzou Daragahi, "The Roots of Hezbollah's Clout Lie in Iran," *Los Angeles Times,* September 10, 2006. Accessed at http://www.latimes.com/news/ printedition/asection/la-fg-lebiran1osep10,1,5703115.story?coll=la-news- a_section.

145. Kathryn Westcott, "Who Are the Hezbollah?" *BBC News,* April 4, 2002. Accessed at http://news.bbc.co.uk/2/hi/middle_east/1908671.stm.

146. Sean Yoong, "Ahmadinejad Destroy Israel, End Crisis," *ABC News,* August 3, 2006. Accessed at http://abcnews.go.com/International/ wireStory?id=2269525.

147. Michael Elliott, "Six Keys to Peace," *Time,* July 31, 2006, p. 33.

148. "Lebanon: The Israel-Hamas-Hezbollah Conflict," *CRS Report for Congress,* August 14, 2006. Accessed at http://www.fas.org/sgp/crs/mid- east/RL33566.pdf.

149. Molly Moore and John Ward Anderson, "Suicide Bombers Change Mid- east's Military Balance," *The Washington Post,* August 18, 2002, pg. A01. Accessed at http://www.washingtonpost.com/ac2/wp-dyn?pagename=ar ticle&contentId=A31236-2002Aug17&notFound=true.

150. "Hezbollah," at http://en.wikipedia.org/wiki/Hezbollah.

151. Rowan Scarborough, "Iran, Hezbollah Support Al-Sadr," *Washington Times,* April 7, 2004. Accessed at http://www.washingtontimes.com/ national/20040407-124311-9361r.htm.

152. Anne Mulrine, "Hell to Pay," *U.S. News & World Report,* September 25, 2006, p. 25.

153. Anderson Cooper, *Dispatches from the Edge: A Memoir of War, Disasters, and Survival* (New York: HarperCollins, 2006), p. 52.

154. "Saddam Hussein arrested in Iraq," *BBC News,* December 14, 2003. Accessed at http://news.bbc.co.uk/2/hi/middle_east/3317429.stm.

155. For information on the Kurds, a discussion beyond the scope of this book, see the insightful *Washington Post* article at http://www.washingtonpost. com/wp-srv/inatl/daily/feb99/kurdprofile.htm.

156. "Saddam Accuser Targets Foreign Arms Merchants," *Reuters News Alert,* September 11, 2006. Accessed at http://www.alertnet.org/thenews/news-desk/COL149437.htm.

157. "Iraq: A Day in the Life of a Normal Iraqi," *Reuters News Alert,* September 11, 2006. Accessed at http://www.alertnet.org/thenews/newsdesk/IRIN/055fe3e8901e65fe36ceof1a211f56ca.htm.

158. Ibid.

159. Stuart Johnson, "Where's Babylon?" Accessed at http://www.leftbehind.com/channelliveforgod.asp?pageid=708&channelID=159.

160. Mark Hitchcock, "Iraqi Democracy and the Future of Babylon," February 3, 2005. Accessed at http://www.leftbehind.com/channelfree.asp?pageid=1101&channelID=175.

161. Ibid.

162. Charles H. Dyer with Angela Elwell Hunt, *The Rise of Babylon* (Wheaton, IL: Tyndale, 1991). Accessed at http://www.jewsforjesus.org/publications/issues/8_1/babylon.

163. As cited at http://www.cnn.com/2006/POLITICS/08/21/bush/index.html.

164. Kenneth Pollack, *The Persian Puzzle* (New York: Random House, 2004), cited at http://joelrosenberg.blogspot.com/2000_06_01_joelrosenberg_archive.html.

165. Scott MacLeod, "We Do Not Need Attacks," *Time,* September 25, 2006, p. 35.

166. Thomas Omestad, "An Impulse for Intrigue," *U.S. News & World Report,* July 31, 2006, p. 35.

167. Michael D. Evans and Jerome R. Corsi, *Showdown with Nuclear Iran* (Nashville, TN: Nelson Current, 2006), p. 17.

168. *Nucleonics Week,* July 3, 2003. Accessed at http://www.tau.ac.il/jcss/nw0307.doc.

169. Sean Yoong, "Ahmadinejad: Destroy Israel, End Crisis," *ABC News,* August 3, 2006. Accessed at http://abcnews.go.com/International/wireStory?id=2269525.

170. William M. Arkin, "Secret Plan Outlines the Unthinkable," *Los Angeles Times,* March 9, 2002. Accessed at http://www.commondreams.org/print.cgi?file=/views02/0309-04.htm.

171. Kenneth M. Pollack, *The Persian Puzzle* (New York: Random House, 2004), p. 345.

172. For a discussion of the definitional problems, see A. William Samii, "Tehran, Washington, and Terror: No Agreement to Differ," *Middle East Review of International Affairs,* vol. 6, no. 3 (September 2002), http://meria. idc.ac.il/journal/2002/issue3/jv6n3a5.html.

173. Mortimer B. Zukerman, "Moscow's Mad Gamble," *U.S. News & World Report,* January 30, 2006, p. 1.

174. Gary Sick, "Confronting Terrorism," *The Washington Quarterly,* Autumn 2003. pp. 83–98. Accessed at http://www.twq.com/03autumn/docs/ 03autumn_sick.pdf.

175. Mark Hitchcock, *Iran: The Coming Crisis* (Sisters, OR: Multnomah, 2006), p. 103.

176. "Fox Facts: Iran's Military Strength," *Fox News,* September 5, 2006. Accessed at http://www.foxnews.com/story/0,2933,211217,00.html.

177. "Iran's Leader Calls for TV Debate with Bush," *CNN News,* August 29, 2006. Accessed at http://www.cnn.com/2006/WORLD/meast/08/29/iran. nuclear/index.html.

178. "Ahmadinejad Pushes for Debate with Bush at U.N.," AP Report, September 6, 2006. Accessed at http://www.foxnews.com/story/0,2933,212505,00. html.

179. Ann Leslie, "Why This Man Should Give Us All Nightmares," *Daily Mail,* August 23, 2006. Accessed at http://www.dailymail.co.uk/pages/live/articles/news/newscomment.html?in_article_id=401858&in_page_id=1787.

180. Joel Rosenberg, *Flash Traffic Update* email subscription, September 6, 2006. Accessible at http://joelrosenberg.blogspot.com.

181. "Iran Turns Away Inspectors," *CNN News,* August 21, 2006. Accessed at http://www.cnn.com/2006/WORLD/meast/08/21/iran.inspectors.ap/ index.html.

182. Joel Rosenberg, *Flash Traffic Update* email subscription, September 7, 2006. Accessed at http://joelrosenberg.blogspot.com.

183. Stu Weber, "Russia and Iran in Bible Prophecy," March 9, 2004. Accessed at http://www.leftbehind.com/channelendtimes.asp?pageid=1276&channelID=71.

184. Cited by Timothy George, "Theology in an Age of Terror," *Christianity Today,* September 2006, p. 78. Accessed at http://www.christianitytoday. com/ct/2006/009/1.78.html.

185. Joel Rosenberg, "Mideast War Spinning Out of Control," July 14, 2006. Accessed at http://www.leftbehind.com/channelfree.asp?pageid=1306&ch

annelID=175. Book cited is *Epicenter: Why current rumblings in the middle east will change your future* (Wheaton, IL: Tyndale, 2006).

186. Joel Rosenberg, "Mideast War Spinning Out of Control," July 14, 2006. Accessed at http://www.leftbehind.com/channelfree.asp?pageid=1306&c hannelID=175.

187. "Moscow Wants to Build 40 to 50 Nuclear Reactors Abroad," *AFX News*, September 7, 2006. Accessed at http://www.sharewatch.com/story. php?storynumber=201429.

188. Ibid.

189. John Thorne, "Putin in Morocco for Middle East Talks," AP News, September 7, 2006. Accessed at http://www.boston.com/news/world/ europe/articles/2006/09/07/russias_putin_in_morocco_to_push_ trade/.

190. George W. Bush, "Address to a Joint Session of Congress and the American People," September 20, 2001. Accessed at http://www.whitehouse. gov/news/releases/2001/09/20010920-8.html.

191. "Israel to Moscow: Hezbollah used Russian-made missiles against IDF," AP News, August 18, 2006. Accessed at http://www.haaretz.com/hasen/ spages/752155.html.

192. Russian Assistance to Iran's Missile Programs," testimony on H.R. 1883, Iran Nonproliferation Act before congressman Dana Rohrabacher, chairman Subcommittee on Space and Aeronautics of the Committee on Science; U.S. House of Representatives, Washington, D.C., July 13, 1999. Accessed at http://www.kentimmerman.com/krt/hsc_testimony.htm.

193. Ken Timmerman, "Missile Threat from Iran," *Readers Digest* exclusive interview, January 1998. Accessed at http://www.kentimmerman.com/krt/ rd_iranmissiles.htm.

194. Ibid.

195. The same congressional testimony notes: "These missiles allow them to target Israel, thus making Iran a 'front-line' state and a direct player in the making of peace or war. They also give Iran the ability to blackmail the United States, and limit our freedom of action in the Persian Gulf."

196. "Nuclear War Starting in 10 Days?" *Pravda*, August 11, 2006. Accessed at http://english.pravda.ru/hotspots/conflicts/11-08-2006/83898-Nuclear_ War-0. Thanks to Dr. Joel Rosenberg for pointing out this source.

197. See Appendix B, "The Nations in Ezekiel 38-39" for details on the identity of these nations.

198. Jon Mark Ruthven, *The Prophecy That Is Shaping History,* cited in Mark Hitchcock, *Iran: The Coming Crisis* (Sisters, OR: Multnomah, 2006), p. 158.

199. Dr. Stu Weber, "Interview with Joel Rosenberg—Part 1," July 7, 2005. Accessed at http://www.leftbehind.com/channelbooks.asp?pageid=1168 &channelID=219.

200. John F. Walvoord, *Israel in Prophecy,* rev. ed. (Grand Rapids, MI: Zondervan, 1962) p. 129.

201. Mark Hitchcock, *Iran: The Coming Crisis* (Sisters, OR: Multnomah, 2006), p. 173.

202. "Russian Assistance to Iran's Missile Programs," testimony on H.R. 1883, Iran Nonproliferation Act before congressman Dana Rohrabacher, chairman Subcommittee on Space and Aeronautics of the Committee on Science U.S. House of Representatives, Washington, D.C., July 13, 1999. Accessed at http://www.kentimmerman.com/krt/hsc_testimony.htm.

203. Ephesians 5:15-16.

204. From the EU's Lisbon Strategy, accessible online at http://ec.europa.eu/ education/policies/2010/et_2010_en.html.

205. International Monetary Fund, World Economic Outlook Database, April 2006. Accessed at http://en.wikipedia.org/wiki/List_of_countries_by_ GDP_%28nominal%29.

206. John F. Walvoord, *Major Bible Prophecies* (Grand Rapids, MI: Zondervan, 1991), pp. 7-8.

207. Mike McLoughlin, "Back to the Future of Missions: The Case for Marketplace Ministry," May 2001. Accessed at http://www.scruples.org/ web/articles/Back%20to%20the%20Future%20of%20Missions%20VI. htm.

208. From the European Wind Energy Association, 2000. Accessed at http:// www.ewea.org/index.php?id=200.

209. John F. Walvoord, *Armageddon, Oil and the Middle East Crisis,* rev. ed. (Grand Rapids, MI: Zondervan, 1990), p. 61.

210. "EU Accuses Israel of 'Disproportionate Use of Force' in Lebanon," *USA Today,* July 13, 2006. Accessed at http://www.usatoday.com/news/ world/2006-07-13-eu-israel_x.htm?csp=34.

211. "Israel Heading for Isolation, Analyst Says," *The Chattanooga Times Free Press,* October 14, 2004, p. A8.

212. According to a 2006 European Commission poll released in the *EU*

Observer, cited at http://www.tiesweb.org/webzine/special_files/israeli_palestinian/index.htm.

213. Robert R. Congdon, "The European Union and the Supra-Religion," paper presented to the 14th Annual Pre-Trib Study Group, Dallas, Texas, December 2005. Accessed at http://www.pre-trib.org/article-view.php?id=253.

214. See www.askelm.org for a map and discussion of this view.

215. Such as in Thomas Ice, "The Emerging Global Community," accessible at http://www.pre-trib.org/article-view.php?id=275.

216. Robert R. Congdon, "The European Union and the Supra-Religion," paper presented to the 14th Annual Pre-Trib Study Group, Dallas, Texas, December 2005. Accessed at http://www.pre-trib.org/article-view.php?id=253.

217. From http://koti.mbnet.fi/neptunia/propheti.htm.

218. J. Hampton Keathley, III, "Foundations for the Study of Prophecy," *Biblical Studies Foundation.* Accessed at http://www.bible.org/page.asp?page_id=1747.

219. George Sweeting, *Today in the Word* (Chicago, IL: Moody Publishing, 1989), p. 40. Cited at http://www.bible.org/illus.asp?topic_id=1190.

220. 2 Peter 1:20-21.

221. 2 Timothy 3:16 NLT.

222. Adapted from J. Hampton Keathley III, "Attitudes or Viewpoints Toward the Bible," *Biblical Studies Foundation.* Accessed at http://www.bible.org/page.asp?page_id=693.

223. Luke 24:25-27.

224. Lehman Strauss, "Bible Prophecy," *Biblical Studies Foundation.* Accessed at http://www.bible.org/page.asp?page_id=412.

225. J. Hampton Keathley III, "Foundations for the Study of Prophecy (Revelation)," *Biblical Studies Foundation.* Accessed at http://www.bible.org/page.asp?page_id=1747.

226. Isaiah 44:6-8.

227. Cited in Lehman Strauss, "Bible Prophecy," *Biblical Studies Foundation.* Accessed at http://www.bible.org/page.asp?page_id=412.

228. Lisa Beamer, in *Christianity Today,* Sept./Oct. 2002. Cited in *Rick Warren's*

Ministry Toolbox, September 6, 2006. Accessed at www.pastors.com/rwmt/?ID=275.

229. 2 Peter 3:13-14.

230. Renald E. Showers, *Maranatha Our Lord, Come!* (Bellmawr, NJ: The Friends of Israel Gospel Ministry, Inc., 1995), p. 17.

231. 1 John 3:2-3.

232. Tim LaHaye, *Revelation Unveiled* (Grand Rapids, MI: Zondervan, 1999), p. 10.

233. 1 John 3:2-3, *The NET Bible,* Biblical Studies Foundation, sn 13. Accessed at http://www.bible.org/netbible/index.htm.

234. Cited in Steve Farrar, *Family Survival in the American Jungle* (Sisters, OR: Multnomah, 1991), p. 48.

235. Renald E. Showers, *Maranatha Our Lord, Come!* (Bellmawr, NJ: The Friends of Israel Gospel Ministry, Inc., 1995), p. 256.

236. Cited in Tim Hansel, *Eating Problems for Breakfast* (Nashville, TN: Word, 1988), p. 33.

237. "Last Days on Earth," transcript of the *20/20* special report aired August 30, 2006. Accessed at http://www.transcripts.tv/.

238. Tim LaHaye, *Are We Living in the End Times?* (Wheaton, IL: Tyndale, 2001), pp. 6-7. Cited at http://www.leftbehind.com/channelendtimes.asp?pageid=510&channelID=71.

239. Quoted by Mark Hitchcock, *Iran: The Coming Crisis* (Sisters, OR: Multnomah, 2006), p. 15.

240. *Pulpit Helps,* December 1987. Survey cited at http://www.limki.com/fruits.doc and http://www.letusreason.org/Current30.htm.

241. "Notional Christians," *The Barna Group.* Accessed at http://www.barna.org/FlexPage.aspx?Page=Topic&TopicID=46.

242. Thanks to http://www.prophecynewswatch.com/ for this reference.

243. "Beliefs: Trinity, Satan," *The Barna Group.* Accessed at http://www.barna.org/FlexPage.aspx?Page=Topic&TopicID=6.

244. Though Dr. Silva is no longer alive, his organization continues to influence many today. For the information on this movement from its source, see their website at http://www.silvamethod.com/sub/subpages/news/ne.html.

245. 2 Timothy 4:3.

246. Bart Ehrman, *Misquoting Jesus* (San Francisco: Harper, 2005); James D. Tabor, *The Jesus Dynasty* (New York: Simon & Schuster, 2006); Garry Wills, *What Jesus Meant* (New York: Viking, 2006); Michael Baigent, *The Jesus Papers* (San Francisco: Harper, 2006); Dan Brown, *The Da Vinci Code* (New York: Doubleday, 2003).

247. Barbara Thiering, *Jesus the Man: Decoding the Real Story of Jesus and Mary Magdalene* (New York: Atria Books, 2006).

248. 2 Timothy 4:3.

249. Noted in *Newsweek,* September 1994.

250. Bill McKibben, "The Christian Paradox," *Harper's Magazine,* August 2005. Accessed at http://www.harpers.org/ExcerptTheChristianParadox.html.

251. 2 Timothy 4:4.

252. *The New York Times,* August 22, 1996, front page.

253. "Only Half of Protestant Pastors Have a Biblical Worldview," *The Barna Group,* January 12, 2004. Accessed at http://www.barna.org/FlexPage. aspx?Page=BarnaUpdate&BarnaUpdateID=156.

254. Statistics from the Family Violence Prevention Fund website, http://www. endabuse.org/resources/facts/.

255. Steve Lansingh, "Film Forum: Of Characters Banished to Hell and Raptured to Heaven," *Christianity Today,* November 16, 2000. Accessed at http://www.christianitytoday.com/ct/2000/146/43.0.html.

256. A survey of *Left Behind*'s readers indicates "nearly 3 in 10 either had unfinished business or didn't want to end their earthly good times just yet." Accessed at http://www.leftbehind.com/channelseekgod.asp?pageid=785 &channelID=6

257. 2 Peter 3:9.

258. Tim LaHaye, *Revelation Unveiled* (Grand Rapids, MI: Zondervan, 2003), p. 112.

259. Charles Ryrie, *Ryrie's Basic Theology,* Electronic Media from Parsons Technology (Chicago: Moddy, 1999).

260. See www.wacriswell.org for information on this influential Christian leader.

261. *Dallas Morning News,* December 22, 2002, posted online at http://www. endtimes.org/walvoord.html.

262. Walvoord's family continues to extend his impact through the John F. Walvoord Student Aid Fund at Dallas Theological Seminary, providing

tuition assistance to future generations of Christian leaders. For more information, please see www.dts.edu/supporters.

263. Zola Levitt, during a 1995 interview for *The John Ankerberg Show* on "What Unparalleled Events Does the Bible Predict Will Encompass the World in the Future?"

264. Randall Price, during the same interview mentioned in the previous endnote.

265. Revelation 3:10.

266. For a broad list of cultural usage, see http://en.wikipedia.org/wiki/Four_Horsemen_of_the_Apocalypse#Cultural_references_to_the_Four_Horsemen_of_the_Apocalypse.

267. Allen Ross, "Messianic Prophecies," *Biblical Studies Foundation.* Accessed at http://www.bible.org/page.php?page_id=2764.

268. Zechariah 12:9-10.

269. Tim LaHaye, as cited in Mark Hitchcock, "America in the End Times." Accessed at http://secure.agoramedia.com/leftbehind/index-leftbehind22.asp.

270. Mark Hitchcock, *Iran: The Coming Crisis* (Sisters, OR: Multnomah, 2006), pp. 120-21.

271. Tim LaHaye, "The Role of the U.S.A. in End Times Prophecy," *Tim LaHaye's Perspective,* August 1999. Accessed at www.timlahaye.com.

272. Special thanks to Dr. Mark Hitchcock, author of *Is America in Bible Prophecy?* (Sisters, OR: Multnomah, 2002), for his help on this section, including his excellent phone interview from which some of this material is adapted.

273. Graham Allison, *Nuclear Terrorism: The Ultimate Preventable Catastrophe* (New York: Owl Books, 2004), p. 12.

274. "Two Years Later, the Fear Lingers," *Pew Research for the People and the Press,* September 4, 2003.

275. Mark Hitchcock, "America in the End Times." Accessed at http://www.leftbehind.com.

276. Matthew 5:13-14.

277. Charles H. Dyer, *The Rise of Babylon: Signs of the End Times* (Wheaton, IL: Tyndale, 1991), p. 168.

278. John Hagee, *Jerusalem Countdown* (Lake Mary, FL: Frontline, 2006), pp. 32-33.

279. These two concepts are developed from Dr. Varner's original articles for Ankerberg Theological Research Institute and are accessible in their original form at http://www.johnankerberg.org/Articles/biblical-prophecy/BP0100W2.htm and http://www.johnankerberg.org/Articles/_PDFArchives/biblical-prophecy/BP4W0899.pdf#search=%22william%20varner%22.

280. His noted work is *Lectures on the Industrial Revolution in England* (Whitefish, MT: Kessinger, paperback edition 2004, originally published 1884).

281. A special thanks to Mr. Dick Dragon for his assistance on the research regarding this area of prophecy in connection with the Jewish marriage tradition as noted in D.A. Miller, *Forbidden Knowledge, Or Is It?* updated expanded ed. (Fountain Valley, CA: Joy Publishing, 1998).

282. As quoted in Dr. William Varner's article "The Promises to Israel." Accessed at http://www.johnankerberg.org/Articles/biblical-prophecy/BP0899W4.htm.

283. John F. Walvoord, *Armageddon, Oil and the Middle East Crisis,* rev. ed. (Grand Rapids, MI: Zondervan, 1990), pp. 227-28.

284. Matthew 5:20.

285. Matthew 5:48.

286. John 3:17.

287. 1 Peter 3:18.

288. 2 Corinthians 5:21.

289. Romans 3:22.

290. Acts 16:31.

291. Romans 10:13.

292. Revelation 3:20.

293. 1 John 5:13.

294. John 1:12.

295. For additional resources, see www.johnankerberg.org.

296. 1 Timothy 2:1-4 NLT.

297. Statistics cited at http://joelrosenberg.blogspot.com.

298. See Acts 4 and Daniel 3 for biblical examples.

299. Broward Liston, "Interview, Missionary Work in Iraq," *Time,* April 13, 2003. Accessed at www.time.com/time/world/article/0,8599,443800,00. html.

300. Ibid.

301. "Who Works Where: Lebanon Latest," Reuters AlertNet, August 24, 2006. Accessed at http://www.alertnet.org/thefacts/reliefresources/115348060912. htm.

302. Charles Swindoll, *Great Attitudes! 10 Choices for Success in Life* (Nashville, TN: Thomas Nelson/Countryman, 2006).

303. Philippians 2:6-8.

304. John F. Walvoord, *End Times* (Nashville, TN: Word Publishing, 1998), pp. 123-24.

305. Charles H. Dyer, *The Rise of Babylon* (Wheaton, IL: Tyndale, 1991).

About the Authors

Dr. John Ankerberg is host of the award-winning apologetics television and radio program *The John Ankerberg Show,* which is broadcast in more than 185 countries worldwide. Founder and president of the Ankerberg Theological Research Institute (ATRI), John has written or cowritten more than 60 books and spoken on Middle Eastern religious issues for more than two decades. Learn more about John's work at johnankerberg.org.

Dillon Burroughs, a full-time writer who has worked with many of today's best-selling authors, is a graduate of Dallas Theological Seminary and holds degrees in both communications and theology. He coauthored *The Da Vinci Code Controversy* with John Ankerberg and serves as a news correspondent for ATRI. Dillon lives with his wife, Deborah, and children, Ben and Natalie, in Indianapolis, Indiana. Discover more at dillonburroughs.org.

Other Harvest House Books by
John Ankerberg, John Weldon, and Dillon Burroughs